HIDE YOUR LOVE AWAY

An Intimate Story Of
BRIAN EPSTEIN
As Told By
LARRY STANTON

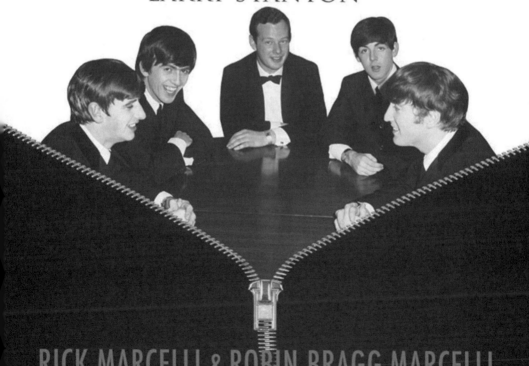

RICK MARCELLI & ROBIN BRAGG-MARCELLI

Cover Design: Jimmy Wachtel

Published by:
Trine Day LLC
PO Box 577
Walterville, OR 97489
1-800-556-2012
www.TrineDay.com
trineday@icloud.com

Library of Congress Control Number: 2020947097

Marcelli, Rick & Bragg-Marcelli, Robin Hide Your Love Away: An Intimate Story of Brian Epstein as told by Larry Stanton—1st ed.
p. cm.

Epub (ISBN-13) 978-1-63424-315-5
Mobi (ISBN-13) 978-1-63424-316-2
HardCover (ISBN-13) 978-1-63424-313-1
TradePaper (ISBN-13) 978-1-63424-314-8

1. Stanton, Laurence (Larry), -- 1933-. 2. Epstein, Brian, -- 1934-1967. 3. Epstein, Brian, -- 1934-1967 -- Friends and associates. 4. Beatles. 5. Music trade -- Great Britain -- History -- 20th century. 6. Kray, Reginald, -- 1933-2000. 7. Kray, Ronald, -- 1933-1995. I. Marcelli, Rick & Bragg-Marcelli, Robin II. Title

First Edition
10 9 8 7 6 5 4 3 2 1

Distribution to the Trade by:
Independent Publishers Group (IPG)
814 North Franklin Street
Chicago, Illinois 60610
312.337.0747
www.ipgbook.com

To our grand children: Djoser, Sienna.

"The love that dare not speak it's name"
                    –Lord Alfred Douglas, Oscar Wilde

TABLE OF CONTENTS

PROLOGUE

O n the last weekend he was alive, Brian Epstein, manager of the
Beatles and the Svengali of a Rock n' Roll Empire, had returned
from his countryside home. Frustrated and depressed about
being stood up by a young man that was supposed to join him for the
Bank Holiday weekend, he decided to return to his Chapel Street home,
hoping that his lover would eventually show up.

Once he was comfortably back home, Brian telephoned Peter Brown,[1]
who was still at his country home in Kingsley Hill in Warbleton, East
Sussex. Brian sounded groggy and tired, and Peter suggested that he return
to Sussex by train and not risk driving alone. He encouraged him to go
back to the country. Peter thought the country air and environment would
do Brian some good. That is why Brian went there in the first place. But he
didn't want to leave his comfortable home and stayed in London. He told
Peter he might go out to some local joints. After all, it was London! Brian
didn't share with Peter that he was hoping someone would be joining him
during the night, a person close to his heart and dear to him.

The year was 1967. On that particular evening, there was an air of
summer warmth that hinted of rain. A soft breeze ruffled the curtains
of the open bedroom windows at Brian's home on 24 Chapel Street,
Belgravia London, England. Brian was engaged in an overseas telephone
conversation with a young and trusted American by the name of Larry
Stanton.

Breaking away from his phone conversation, Brian told Larry to
hold on for a moment because he thought he heard someone in the
hallway outside of his bedroom. Larry heard Brian call out, "Is someone
there?" After a moment and with no response, he continued his phone
conversation, nervously saying he must be losing his mind. Turning away
from the bedroom door, he kept talking to Larry.

Unbeknownst to Brian, a visitor stood in the shadows of the dimly lit
bedroom just outside the door. This mysterious visitor peered through

---

1. Peter Brown was one of Brian Epstein's personal assistant and friends during the 1960's, and
continued to work for the Beatles Apple Corps after Epstein's death. Brown had been rejected by his
Catholic family due to his homosexuality and was greatly influenced by Epstein's success in business.

the smoke-filled bedroom at Brian lying on a rather large comfortable bed, propped up by multiple pillows. Suddenly the conversation stopped, and Larry heard what seemed like someone else talking to Brian. Brian sounded startled, as Larry listened to the sound of muffled voices as if Brian had covered the phone with his hand.

Larry struggled to hear what he could. Just as the phone sounded like it had dropped to the floor, he heard the chilling phrase, "Oh my God," followed by a distinct "I thought you..." The phone line went dead, and the only sound was the dial tone. For a minute or two, he stayed on the phone, hoping Brian would come back, but the finality of the tone told him otherwise.

The next day, when Brian hadn't surfaced, his housekeeper Antonio tried to call Peter Brown to see if he had talked to Brian. However, Peter was not reachable since he was in a local pub with Geoffrey Ellis.[2] Later in the day, Peter telephoned Epstein at his home number, which coincidently was at the precise time a doctor arrived to check up on Epstein. Peter Brown was still holding on the line as Brian Epstein was discovered dead, lying on the bed in his room.

During the last year of Brian's life, the Sexual Offenses Act 1967 was in the process of amending the laws of England and Wales relating to the decriminalization of homosexual acts. Unfortunately, for Brian Epstein, it wasn't soon enough.

You are about to read a story that has been kept secret for decades, until now.

---

2. Geoffrey Ellis worked closely with the Beatles and manager Brian Epstein during the sixties, ended his illustrious career at PRS for Music, and passed away at age 87. During a thirty-five year career in the music business, Ellis became a key figure in running the business affairs of the Fab Four, as well as artists Gerry & The Pacemakers, Billy J. Kramer & the Dakotas, Cilla Black, and Elton John.

CHAPTER ONE

THE BEATLES ARE COMING

In February of 1963, a young twenty-six-year-old California native by the name of Larry Stanton was having a midnight dinner at Tiny Naylor's drive-in, a prime example of Goodie architecture and curbside service on La Brea and Sunset Blvd. in Hollywood, California. Sitting next to him in his convertible sports car was his roommate Jerry Walker. Suddenly over the AM radio, they heard the Beatles song "Please, Please, Me." Both were thrilled when the Beatles hit played over the car radio for the first time. In a world where the Beach Boys, Four Seasons, and the Supremes were the popular music, this new sound really got them excited. They kidded about having the chance to meet the Beatles someday and laughed about it. If only dreams could come true. Soon every teenager would have the same conscious awakening and the same dream.

The Beatles manager, Brian Epstein, was leading the way of what would soon be called Beatlemania. Never before had a British rock band been so popular here in the U.S.A. And due to Brian Epstein and the Beatles, all of this was changing. Brian was at the forefront of historical changes in music. No one could have imagined that the Beatles would influence changes in popular music and fashion that would affect this and future generations worldwide.

Several months before the Beatles arrived in America, a terrible tragedy occurred; John F. Kennedy, the 35th President, had been assassinated. Those gunshots instantly crushed the promise of the American dream, and the country spiraled into despair. When the Beatles arrived in February 1964, they brought a freshness and innocence that lifted Americans from the depression they had been living with. Brian Epstein's timing could not have been better.

The Beatles were heard over car radios everywhere, and that contributed to the recovery of our national spirit. As if that wasn't enough, Brian had booked the Beatles on the most-watched television show in America, the Ed Sullivan Show. Our lives, and certainly that of Larry's, would never be the same. Beatlemania had arrived, and tens of thousands of young screaming teenage girls and boys were there to prove it.

Besides Brian working his magic, making the Beatles and other artists he represented known around the world, he was on a secret quest to fulfill his personal love life and desires. And in Los Angeles, our young Californian Larry is in search of his own fulfilling career and meaningful relationship. Both men had no choice but to search for love in a secret world. For Brian, it was as if the more successful he became, the lonelier he was.

Little did Brian know that a person would come into his life over the next year that would change his life in ways he could never have predicted! And little did Larry know that meeting Brian would change his life. After all, we all are looking for love, that one person we can truly trust and love for the rest of our lives. The question was if that is even possible.

CHAPTER TWO

MEET LARRY AND DIZ

H ollywood is known all over the world as the capital of entertainment. It's recognized for its celebrities, movie stars, powerbrokers, and unequaled insincerity. Far from being the City of Angeles, the tinsel town community is more synonymous with the sinister side of life. Hollywood is more of a place full of double-talk, double standards, double dipping, and double-dealing back-stabbers. But, it can be rewarding to those that make the sacrifices to become rich, powerful, and famous. Most people come to Hollywood in search of their dreams, and end up selling their soul. Regardless of the circumstance, Hollywood can be magical.

Larry Stanton didn't come to Hollywood chasing a dream; he was born and raised in Los Angeles, a true native of California. He went to good public schools, grew up exploring the city with friends, joined the Air Force, and, like so many others in Hollywood, had aspirations of becoming a successful singer. For a brief but celebrated moment in his life, Larry had acquired a contract with Henry "Hank" Sanicola, who signed him to Reprise records. Hank was a music manager and publisher, best known for his work and association with Frank Sinatra. Sadly, none of Larry's recordings were ever released. Over time he realized he had to work hard to pay the rent. It's impressive that he never gave up his dream; great things could happen to him if he just kept moving forward. After all, success could be just around the next corner. Even today, in 2020, Larry is optimistic and still has dreams to hold on to.

In early 1964 Larry Stanton was singing at Shelly's Manne-Hole,[1] one of Hollywood's popular jazz clubs. Shelly's was a hangout for jazz musicians, music lovers, and recording sessions players, like the famous Wrecking Crew.[2] After

1. Shelly's Manne-Hole was located at 1608 Cahuenga Blvd. in Hollywood.
2. The Wrecking Crew was a collective group of session musicians based in Los Angeles whose services were employed for thousands of studio recordings in the 1960s and early 1970s. They played on several

working at places like Gold Star Studios, Valentine Recording Studios, and Western Recorders, they would head straight to Shelly's to unwind. Shelly Manne was one of the best drummers in the music business, and he took a big liking to Larry. Shelly enjoyed giving new talent a shot at fame and would help just about anyone talented and ambitious.

One evening, after Larry finished his set, he decided to leave the club, so he opened the exit door and walked out. The place was called Cosmo's Alley. His red 1957 shabby looking Fiat 'Spyder' convertible sports car was parked in the alley. Leaning on the vehicle and waiting was his roommate Gerald "Jerry" Walker. Jerry was one of two roommates living with Larry. Next to Jerry was a friend that unexpectedly showed up. Jerry introduced him as his friend Diz. His real name was John Gillespie, but he went by the nickname of Diz. Not to be confused with jazz trumpeter John Birks "Dizzy" Gillespie.

Diz came to Hollywood because he too had high hopes of becoming an actor. Larry couldn't help but notice that Diz had movie-star good looks. Jerry told Larry they were both inside the club in time to catch his set. Jerry praised his singing style and performance. Diz nodded assuredly while giving Larry a round of applause. He noticed that Diz was a little too flattering and appeared to be championing the skills of insincerity. Perhaps Larry's insecurities were getting in the way of accepting a genuine compliment. Larry thanked them both with a gracious bow and humbly told Jerry, he had the next shift at the Yellow Cab Company and need to get over there quickly. Jerry asked if he would like to meet up with them later, for a drink or a bite to eat, and Larry said, "Sure, but where?"

"Let's meet at Dino's Lodge on the Sunset Strip. Around 1:30 A.M." With all in agreement, Larry hopped into his car and drove down the alley. He thought to himself that Diz looked like trouble.

He arrived at Dino's Lodge[3] around 1:05 A.M. and spotted Jerry and Diz sitting in a booth overlooking a spectacular nighttime view of Los Angeles's twinkling lights. They could see as far away as the Inglewood Oil fields. Jerry and Diz

hundred top hits. Though not publicly recognized they were viewed with prestige by industry insiders.
3. Dino's Lodge was a popular spot originally owned by Dean Martin and his partner Maure Sammuels. There was a large cartoon neon sign with Dean Martin's face on it that made the location easy to identify. Dino's Lodge was located at 8524 Sunset Blvd. It was right next to the fictional 77 Sunset Strip detective offices

were both enjoying a smoke and cocktails as Larry slid smoothly into the booth. The interior décor at Dino's Lodge included dark wood paneling and comfortable leather booths meant to replicate Dean Martin's[4] personal den.

A separate cocktail lounge provided continuous entertainment that promoted female singers. Perhaps ole Dino didn't want any male competition. Jerry, Diz, and Larry, while relishing their late-night meal, were having a great conversation about their dreams and goals. Larry got an uneasy feeling from Diz, leading Larry to believe Diz didn't care what he had to do to earn money. His attitude and comments were on the order of "there's a sucker born every minute."

"One thing you can always say about Los Angeles is that it's beautiful," said Larry. They each raised their drink to toast, thankful for living in Hollywood. Larry asked Diz what he was doing to earn money while he was living in Hollywood, and how long he planned on staying. Diz said he was getting money from his parents in Ohio because they think he's attending UCLA. He explained that further education wasn't where his interest lay. All he wanted to be was an actor.

"So, your parents think you're going to UCLA as a full-time student?" Diz laughed and said, "The only thing I'm getting from UCLA is a great LSD connection."

Diz explained to them that LSD stood for Lysergic Acid Diethylamide, a very potent hallucinogenic drug. It's a psychedelic drug known for its psychological effects that may include altered awareness of one's surroundings, perceptions, and feelings. It provides sensations and images that seem real, though they are not. He admitted to both of them that his connection was an assistant that worked for an Associate Professor at UCLA. Diz suggested they should try "acid," another name used for LSD. But Larry declared, "No, I would never want to take that kind of drug. It seems dangerous and scary."

"Not true," said Diz, "Only if you have a bad trip, is it scary. It can open your thoughts and allow you to see the world differently. If you have good thoughts in your head, the hallucinations are great." Diz grinned and said with a sly look and cunning voice, "Time will tell if you ever try it or not. It's a real mind opening and happening drug. If either of you wants to try it, I would love to turn you on."

---

4. Dean Martin was born Dino Paul Crocetti on June 7, 1917 and died December 25, 1995. He was an actor, comedian and singer. Also known as the "King of Cool" and early on partnered with Jerry Lewis as one of the most successful comedy teams. Dino was a close friend to Frank Sinatra and part of the Rat Pack.

They said good-bye and Larry told Jerry he would see him at home. Larry wasn't sure where Diz was staying while in Los Angeles, but Jerry was going to drop him off somewhere before going home.

On Larry's drive home, thoughts kept rumbling through his head. As much as he trusted Jerry, he had an unsettling feeling about Diz Gillespie, but he just couldn't put his finger on it. Maybe it was because Diz was lying to his parents, using them and misleading them. All Diz spoke about was his attempts at an acting career and using people to score drugs like LSD. If Diz could deceive his parents, he could deceive just about anyone. As the sun started to rise from the west, the streets glistened with morning dew wetness.

CHAPTER THREE

LARRY THE CROONER

A cross the country, Brian Epstein boarded a jet airliner flight from New York to Los Angeles. Brian had just finished up another day of business. It was customary for Brian to pay for all his travel expenses himself, not charging back his clients, so trips were split partially between business and personal. When the plane landed, he collected his bags, and as there was no waiting limo, he hailed a Yellow Cab to take him to his hotel.

The following night, Larry was once again performing at Shelly's Manne-Hole and loving every minute of it. As usual, Shelly was hugely supportive and encouraged Larry to keep working at his singing and stage presence. Little did Larry know, but Shelly had a surprise that night for him. He had invited Hank Sanicola[1] to come down to listen to the singers perform that evening. When the set ended, Larry took a bow and exited towards the back bar. Shelly motioned him over and told Larry he wanted to introduce someone. "Larry, I'd like you to meet Hank Sanicola," said Shelly. While shaking his hand, Larry conveyed how happy he was to meet him. As it turned out, this introduction resulted in Hank signing Larry to a Reprise Record contract.

Feeling exhausted, Larry planned on going home for the evening to catch up on some much-needed sleep. He said good night to the house band "The Quintet," then he gave Shelly a hug and a heartfelt "thank you." Leaving through the back door, he got into his car and put his key into the ignition. All he heard was a rapid clicking sound; the engine wouldn't turn over. Once Larry pushed the clutch down, it started to roll, and once it started moving, he popped the clutch. He steered it down the alley and continued off towards home and into a comfortable bed. Sweet dreams!

The next day, Larry drove through Hollywood to West Los Angeles and straight over to the Yellow Cab Taxi garage for work. Looking straight ahead through his windshield, it appeared to be one of those typical Hollywood evenings, with the city's twinkling lights and pumping energy.

1. Henry W. "Hank Sanicola was born on June 14 1914 and died October 1,97, he was an American music manager, publisher, businessman and pianist, best known for his work and associations with Frank Sinatra from the late 1930's to the early 1960's

There were characters out searching for borderline illegal activity, and normal, boring types.

Most were in the seedier parts of Hollywood and Los Angeles, where underground bars and darkened alleys offered temptations of all kinds. He came across both male and female fares looking for prostitutes, cross dressers, guys looking to go to strip joints, and those requesting lesbian or gay bars (which was illegal at the time). Also, he got those out looking to score drugs. Larry knew where the offbeat places were.

After dropping off a fare close to the garage, he decided to drive over there to see how the other drivers were doing. Matt, one of his fellow cab drivers motioned for Larry to come over to him so he could say something in private. Matt could barely hold back his excitement in telling Larry that he had picked up a fare that was throwing a party at a private hotel bungalow in Beverly Hills. The fare extended the party invitation to him and any friends he wanted to bring along. Matt told Larry he wanted him

to go and had already invited Jerry Walker and his friend from Ohio. Larry was a bit surprised that Matt called Jerry, but went along with the saying "the more, the merrier." What the cab driver didn't tell Larry was that the fare he dropped off at The Beverly Hills Hotel[2] was none other than Brian Epstein, the manager of the Beatles.

Going to an elegant party at the Beverly Hills Hotel, with the possibility of meeting different types of people, should prove to be one heck of a good time! Where else can this type of opportunity happen … only in Hollywood!

Matt grabbed a pencil and paper from a nearby table and scribbled Beverly Hills Hotel, Bungalow 6A.

---

2. The Beverly Hills Hotel was also known at the Pink Palace. Its located in Beverly Hills on Sunset Blvd. It's decorated in the peachy pink and green colors, which are a trademark of the hotel. In 2012 the hotel was named the first historic landmark in Beverly Hills. Many celebrities stayed at the hotel from Howard Hughes, Elizabeth Taylor, Marilyn Monroe, Marlene Dietrich, John Lennon and Yoko and Brian Epstein. Recently George Clooney has been calling for an immediate boycott of the luxury hotel owned now by the Sulton of Brunei; he is reacting to the enactment of laws that make it potentially legal to murder gay people by stoning them.

CHAPTER FOUR

A PARTY IN HOLLYWOOD

L arry lived in the heart of Hollywood just off of Vine Street in a gray and white 1928 Mediterranean style duplex that was right on the corner of El Centro and De Longpre. Larry had two roommates, Gerald "Jerry" Walker and Art Eisner. It was a necessary arrangement for each of them to afford to live in Hollywood. Before Larry ran out the front door, Jerry told him he was going to pick up Diz, and they would meet him later on at the party. "That sounds great. It ought to be a good time for all of us." He told Jerry he was going to stop and get something to eat before going to the party. He proceeded to drive towards Fountain Avenue heading west, and continued about three miles before hanging a left on La Cienaga Blvd. The route he planned to take meant he would need to make a right hand turn on Santa Monica Blvd., which he did. He then continued his drive going west along the road with the train tracks on his

left that separated the east and west lanes. While continuing the drive west bound he turned right going north on San Vicente boulevard, and then zoomed to Sunset where he hung a left turn and continued west on Sunset. He quickly moved over to the right hand lane when he saw the place he would like to grab a meal and felt lucky to see a parking spot right in front of the Hamburger Hamlet restaurant.[1]

1. The Hamburger Hamlet opened in 1950 at 8931 Sunset Blvd. down the block from the Whiskey A Go-Go Club. Marilyn Lewis, a Hollywood Costumer and her husband Harry who was an actor best known for his role in

The Hamburger Hamlet was one of Larry's favorite places to eat on the Sunset Strip. He knew he could always get a great hamburger, and would often get a burger to go just so he could enjoy eating it at home and being messy in private. Larry's thoughts rushed back to what lay ahead of him at the party. Most patrons of the Beverly Hills Hotel were either very wealthy or a celebrity. His curiosity and fantasies would be satisfied very soon.

It was around 11:00 P.M., and Larry assumed the party would be well underway. He hoped some of the people he knew were already there, but if not, he could always rely on his charm. Larry jumped in his car and headed west down Sunset. In the distance, he saw a Beverly Hills City Limits sign indicating that he was getting close to the hotel. As he drove past that iconic sign, he entered into what  seemed to be another world, a world called Beverly Hills,[2] land of the rich and famous. The Beverly Hills Hotel was directly in front of his view as he turned right on Crescent Drive. He looked for a parking spot and saw one on the left, so he made a U-turn and parked his car. The sun had set about an hour before he left the garage, and there was a red glow hovering over the edge of blackness in the skies of greater Los Angeles.

The full moon revealed itself and seemed to light his way from above as he walked the hotel pathway from the street to the bungalows. The sound of crickets clicking their legs seemed to fill the night. Larry laughed to himself because there were times the sound of crickets sounded just like zippers being unzipped. That would depend, of course, how close you were to the zipper.

Following the sounds of music and laughter, he came upon Bungalow #6A. He opened the door and walked in. Larry took a glance, hoping to see a friendly face. Initially, he didn't see anyone he recognized. He had no idea what he had walked into or even who the host of the party was.

Immediately he noticed there were no women at the party and thought what a pleasant surprise. Larry was offered a joint by an out of work actor, whose face looked familiar, but he couldn't think of his name. Scattered

---

Humphrey Bogart film "Key Largo" created this well-liked hamburger restaurant, its original idea for it to be an actor's hangout

2. Beverly Hills was and still is considered to be an affluent city of Los Angeles, California. Beverly Hills was incorporated in 1914. At the time restrictions prohibited non-whites from owning or renting property unless employed as servants by white residents. It was also forbidden to sell or rent property to Jews in Beverly Hills. In 1925 Beverly Hills bought 385 acres for a new university campus, UCLA. By 1940 successful black actors and businessmen began to move into Beverly Hills, despite the covenants unenforceable in 1948 in Shelly v Kramer.

around and ready for consumption were all sorts of pills, liquor, and large amounts of pot. As Larry stood there casing the room, he suddenly felt a sudden tap on his shoulder that made him turn around with a whip of his head. He was face-to-face with a handsome dark-haired man wearing a V-neck cashmere sweater, slick pressed slacks, and dark leather shoes.

Larry was taken by surprise when the man spoke, with such a proper British accent. He introduced himself as Brian Epstein. Larry quickly responded that his name is Loren Stanton, but his friends call him Larry. The next few words out of Brian's mouth were, "You sure have beautiful eyes, Lauren." He took that as a compliment but knew it was also a form of flirtation. He immediately knew who the man was after he revealed his name. The name Brian Epstein was almost as well known as the names of the Beatles.

Now that Larry knew who the host of the party was, he was equally excited about sharing more conversations with the famous Mr. Brian Epstein. Standing in the room was the man responsible for making The Beatles rock stars. Under his belt as well and continuing on the rise were Gerry and the Pacemakers, Cilla Black, and Billy J. Kramer with the Dakotas. Once again, Larry looked around the room, and this time focused on observing the action and noticed the body language of party attendees. He spotted some rather important people in the entertainment industry. Among them were some well-known musicians and composers. "Wow," he thought," impressive!"

In one corner, he saw Lionel Bart,[3] who was throwing back a drink of gin while sitting at a piano, tapping out some musical notes to one of his famous tunes. Other party guests casually leaned against the piano chiming in and singing show tunes along with Lionel. The room was filled with laughter and the sound of glasses clinking. There was a thin mist of cigarette and pot smoke hovering close to the ceiling like the smog that engulfs Los Angeles.

Brian stood in place, admiring Larry with his slick James Dean look. Even though it was a different style from the way he dressed, it looked

---

3. Lionel Bart, Andrew Lloyd Weber once described Lionel Bart as "the Father of modern British musical." Lionel Bart won a Tony for the Best Original Score for "Oliver." The film version won a total of 6 Academy Awards, including Best Picture. Other compositions Lionel wrote were the theme song to the James Bond film "From Russia with Love," and songs for Cliff Richards and Shirley Bassey. He was known for his outlandish lifestyle, celebrity friends, and the overindulgence in his outrageous parties. While "Oliver" was performing in the West End in London he and the show were just down the street from his friend Brian Epstein's offices. They also lived near each other in England. Lionel was a writer and composer of British pop music and musicals and was largely responsible for the birth of British pop. He was Jewish and gay and shared those same qualities with Brian and the reason a strong reason for their shared friendship.

great on Larry. Trying to conceal it, Larry felt the eyes of attention on him. Brian said he never wore Levi jeans, as his style was, as one would say, different in England. That was just another way of describing his style as conservative. Brian's preference in attire was to wear dress slacks, long sleeve shirts or sweaters, and black shoes. He was very picky, yes, when it came to his attire and image. Brian was known to wear expensive suits, monogrammed silk shirts, and he drove an expensive car.

It wasn't long before he realized Brian was very conventional and conservative in appearance, but not so traditional in his social life and sexual preferences. Brian politely excused himself to talk to his other guests mingling in the room. He wanted to make sure all his other guests felt welcomed; it was essential to participate in all the entertainment chatter.

Brian Epstein's bungalow was a one-bedroom suite, very spacious, nicely decorated, and nestled amongst the blooming bougainvillea. The tropical palms provided extra privacy. The suite ambiance was comfortable and inviting. Add to that a lovely burning fireplace, and you get the romantic atmosphere perfect for getting to know one another. Acres of tropical gardens and exotic flowers surrounded the bungalow suites. On that night, it seemed as if Larry and Brian were the only people in the room. A smooth and comforting tone in Brian's soft voice made Larry feel special. As the night progressed, Larry felt this could be the start of something special, very special. Once Brian and Larry started to open up to one another, their conversation became revealing and set a tone for the days ahead.

They talked for hours, babbling on as if they were two girls at a high school slumber party. The age difference between them was about four years, with Brian being older. They had no problem finding common ground and similar interests. Brian admitted that he smoked weed, drank alcohol, and popped pills when needed. "In reality, it was John Lennon that introduced me to pills," said Brian. He continued talking about drugs and John, but then caught himself and stopped. In a soft voice, he asked Larry to keep that little piece of information between them. Larry nodded his head in agreement and said, "No problem, I understand." His hand swept across his mouth as if closing a zipper. "My lips are sealed." At that moment, Brian's intuition told him that Larry was a person he could trust, and Larry knew that because he told him afterward. Brian's hand softly touched Larry's shoulder as he thanked him. His touch sent tingling sensations throughout Larry's body.

While both continued talking away on the couch, a very attractive and sophisticated looking young man walked over to where Brian and Larry sat. Larry looked up to see it was none other than John "Diz" Gillespie. Diz asked Larry to introduce him to his friend and party host. Anyone noticing could see that Brian took a long hard second look at Diz. Standing there with such a good build, he was thin but not skinny, about 5'10" in height, with dark thick wavy hair. Diz looked at Brian with bright, piercing eyes. When Larry introduced the two, Larry noticed they held hands a little longer than a normal handshake.

Larry felt a twinge of jealousy, although there was no reason for him to feel that way as he and Brian just met. Perhaps it was due to the liquor and pot that distorted his thoughts and feelings. Diz slowly released his grip, as if teasing Brian, and then said, "What a pleasure it is to meet you, Brian, and thank you for having such a great party." Diz slowly walked away like the stud he was, stating he should mingle and meet other people at the party. His strut was also a tease for Brian.

Brian turned towards Larry and said, "Your friend is very charming and interesting. What a good looking man!" Larry only shook his head yes in agreement. It wouldn't be the last time Brian would see Diz Gillespie, and in time it would become apparent how domineering he would become in Brian's life. Larry felt a moment of regret. It's as if a little voice in his ear was saying to him, "Watch out for that guy! Guys like him have only one thing in mind, and it isn't to make someone else happy."

CHAPTER FIVE

THE TOUCH

The party continued into the early morning hours. As morning approached, several guests paired up and slowly left the party. Lionel Bart, having decided to call it a night at Brian's, voiced he was going to continue with a party at his house. Larry couldn't help but laugh out loud and said, "That Lionel Bart knows how to enjoy life!" Lionel flamboyantly gestured a farewell to Brian, then slowly turned around and left with a small group of attractive young men. But not before taking an extravagant finale bow as if on a West End theatre in London.

After Lionel left the bungalow, Brian's attention turned to Larry. Brian was interested in getting to know Larry a little more rather than going to Lionel's house to engage in another never-ending party. They continued to talk and laugh, fully engaged with each other, oblivious to time, everyone, and anything else going on around them. In a moment of intimacy, Brian touched Larry's leg with his hand that sent a chill through Larry's body. It was a moment of pure sexual excitement that tickled his insides. At that moment, they realized there was something else they had in common. That commonality was a sexual preference for men. They discussed the dangers of being gay and how difficult it was to keep it a secret. It was a solemn moment, but they quickly moved past it.

Another topic that came up was religion. Brian and Larry revealed that they were Jewish. Brian, with a sad face, talked about how he struggled with being Jewish and gay. Larry admitted he had the same problem and struggled with those issues. After all, it was illegal to be gay in the U.S. and England. Most gay people had to go underground to let loose, be free, and be who they truly were. Love was something you had to hide away. Larry felt Brian's pain and reached over to pull Brian closer, giving him a big hug.

Within that hidden world were the rich and powerful people who were homosexuals but stayed in the closet. There were powerful gay men who used blackmail and extortion, preying on other gay men for their financial gain. Brian told Larry about the Kray twins, a couple of business mobsters who were making a lot of noise in England. They were rumored to be gay and on the way to becoming notorious gangsters. Those were the types to be wary of, and it scared Brian. He had to explain this to Larry, as he had no idea who the Kray twins were. Later in their relationship, he found out more than he needed to know about the infamous sociopathic killers, the Kray twins.

CHAPTER SIX

THE SLEEPOVER

In 2020, it's hard for most to imagine that homosexuality was still illegal during the '60s, and how gays had to live with their secrets. Homosexuals and lesbians were outcasts. If their secrets were exposed, they could be fired from jobs, kicked out of their homes, and even arrested. Brian and Larry were two of those lost souls. As Larry carefully listened, Brian confided how he wished with all his heart to find true love. To do business with the "big boys," Brian Epstein became part of a secret world, a world of powerful men, and a kind of mafia…. A "Velvet Mafia."

The party's bartender walked up to them, and politely said, "Sir, I think its time for me to go." Brian looked around the dimly lit room and realized almost everyone had left. Brian graciously thanked the bartender and asked him if he would be so kind as to wake the stragglers and show them the way out. The bartender gladly agreed. Brian stepped away from Larry for a moment so he could get cash to pay the bartender. Upon his return, Brian stopped Larry from leaving and said, "Well, if he is going to be leaving us now, let's indulge in another nightcap."

Both lost control of how much they had been drinking up to that point. Brian got up and poured them both another drink then lit up a joint and offered it to Larry. The joint was accepted as he took in a deep drag of the neatly rolled pot. Becoming higher with each puff, they seemed to get physically closer while they sat together on the couch. Their bodies seemed to be melting into one being.

Suddenly they realized it was 5:00 A.M. and they should probably catch a little sleep and call it a night. They both looked swiftly around the room and saw the early morning sunlight bleeding through the Venetian blinds like an unwelcome visitor. The fragrance of jasmine started to fill the room along with a chill from an opened window. There were still a few party guests in the corner of the bungalow that the bartender had overlooked. Brian shrugged his shoulders and gestured with a motion, "Shhh … Lets not disturb them." He was confident they would show themselves out when they woke up.

Brian walked over and opened the double doors that led to his spacious and beautiful bedroom so he could get prepared for bed. Turning to Larry, he said, "You're welcome to stay." He offered to share his bed since it was large and beckoning for the company. Larry felt a little shy but flattered at the same time. He knew he shouldn't drive in his stoned and drunk condition. He struggled with what to say and didn't respond immediately, but then replied, "Sure, that does sound inviting!" He told Brian he would crash for just a few hours, as he needed to go home and get prepared for another day of work.

He managed to stagger over to the window just as the sun became impossible to bear, closed the window and blinds, and shut the blackout curtains. He walked over to the bedroom door, where Brian stood waiting patiently with a look of desire in his eyes. Larry thought to himself, "after all, when in Rome, do as the Romans do." Larry followed, as Brian gently closed the doors behind them.

CHAPTER SEVEN

THE MORNING AFTER

When Larry woke up, he was alone in bed. It was around 11:00 A.M. in the late morning. At least he'd gotten a few hours of sleep, he thought to himself and felt pretty good considering. For a brief moment, when he woke up, he wondered where he was. Looking around, Larry noticed the room was dark, and he was stark naked. As he sat up in bed, he heard a noise from the other side of the bedroom door. Brian was already awake and dressed without Larry hearing any of it. Larry got out of bed and grabbed a towel from the bathroom. He must have been totally out of it and in a deep sleep. He guessed that came within moments of satisfaction.

Larry opened the bedroom doors and walked out to see Brian sitting on a stool in the kitchen already dressed in a crisp white dress shirt, a lovely blue tie, and pressed pair of dark slacks. Sitting next to him was a service tray with a bright yellow fresh grapefruit sitting on top of a quaint little plate with a silver spoon.

Brian saw Larry and said, "Good morning to you. Go have a shower, and I'll make you a cup of good English tea." Larry took a quick look around the bungalow and saw they were all alone. The other guests that had been there when they went to bed must have let themselves out during the early morning. After showering, he joined Brian.

Larry said good-morning as he sat down at the kitchen table with Brian. He marveled over how fresh Brian's appearance seemed to be, almost glowing. Larry felt a little embarrassed by having on the same clothes and looking like a guy who stayed up all night having too much fun. In reality, he was just that, a guy that stayed up all night having too much fun! Brian had a full day's work ahead of him with several appointments to attend. Larry's appearance was the last thing Brian was concerned with; it didn't bother him at all.

During their brief morning breakfast chat Brian was so sweet as he offered more tea. Larry replied, "No, thank you. I have to go home and freshen up to get ready for another day of work." Larry asked shyly, "Can we see each other again?" Brian acknowledged by saying, "Absolutely!

You beat me to the request. Will you please give me your telephone number?" Brian passed a piece of paper to Larry that already had his hotel telephone number and home number in the U.K. Larry jotted down his phone number and address before passing it over to Brian. Brian whipped out his little black book and immediately copied the numbers into his private little phone book. In 2019 Brian's telephone/address book was being sold, and it still had Lauren Stanton's information written by hand, Hollywood address, and all. The exchange of contact information made both of them feel happy to realize there could be another get-together, and hopefully, who knew what else.

Larry ran his hand through his thick brown hair and said to Brian, "I look forward to seeing you again, but do know that if it doesn't happen for some reason or another, I've enjoyed your company." Looking into Larry's eyes, Brian said, "I want it to continue; I truly mean that Lauren." Larry walked over to Brian and gave him a big hug while whispering in his ear, "Please call me Larry." He turned and walked out, slowly closing the door behind him. The minute he closed the door, Larry wondered what Brian's thoughts might be about him. Larry had hoped that the glowing look on Brian's face had something to do with the wonderful evening they shared.

CHAPTER EIGHT

DINE & DASH

I t was another one of those beautiful sunny mid-morning days in Beverly Hills as Larry made his way to his car. Larry reached into his jacket pocket and found his Ray-Ban sunglasses, so necessary to combat the glaring California sunlight. He hopped in, and amazingly, it started right up. He proceeded to drive his Fiat down Sunset Boulevard towards the Sunset Strip. Larry was in a state of euphoria with thoughts about the special night and what the future might hold for him and his new friend.

Larry felt as if he was floating on cloud nine. Could it all be a dream? He turned on the A.M. radio in his car only to hear the Beatles music blast out, "I Want to Hold Your Hand." From that moment on, there wouldn't be a Beatles song he heard that wouldn't trigger fond memories of Brian and the night they first met and shared time such magical moments together. The way Larry talked to Brian, the subtle expressions and use of sexual innuendos, seemed to entice Brian even more. Larry realized that he knew Brian's secret, his very private secret.

Once Larry arrived home at his duplex in Hollywood, he checked the mailbox, rushed into his apartment, peeled off his clothes, and took another shower. Afterward, he felt new energy running through his veins as if he had slept for eight hours. With renewed energy, Larry went about his daily routine that included contacting his music industry contacts to secure the next singing gig. Even though he wanted to tell the world what had happened and whom he had met the night before, he decided to be close-lipped about it for the time being. As the saying goes, loose lips sink ships!

He kept in touch with people in the recording industry as well as in the auto business. He contacted dealerships hoping one of them might be interested in a new salesperson. The calls took about thirty minutes to complete. He would do any type of work to make a buck, as long as it was legal.

With business over, Larry's stomach started to growl so loud he was sure it could be heard across the room. A slight hangover had crept into his head after last night's party romp. He left the apartment rather quickly and drove straight over to Schwab's Pharmacy[1] on Sunset Blvd. Not only was

1. Schwab's Pharmacy was located on Sunset Blvd. and Crescent Heights Blvd. in the heart of what is now knows as West Hollywood

Schwab's one of his favorite places, but it was also a landmark icon from a by-gone era of Hollywood's history. Many struggling actresses were discovered at Schwab's. It was located a few feet east of Crescent Heights and the Pandora's Box.[2]

Larry walked into Schwab's, grabbed the *Hollywood Reporter,* *Daily Variety,* and *Billboard* magazine from the front counter and slid into the seat at his regular booth. He quickly ordered breakfast and coffee. By the time he finished breakfast, Larry had read most of the papers. He also knew the Beatles had 14 songs on the *Billboard Hot 100* singles chart for the year. After he wiped his plate clean with the last bite of toast and the last sip of coffee,

Larry reached into his pocket for money and realized he was short of cash. He left what money he had on the table for a tip. Larry thought, "How could I have left the apartment without all my money?" The only thing he could do was to leave as discreetly as possible. He walked over to the counter and grabbed another copy of the *Daily Variety* paper, slipping the breakfast check between the pages. He walked towards the register and paid for the trade magazine but not the breakfast, then left Schwab's. Larry mumbled, "Some days you got it, and some days you have to improvise."

Realizing he was too tired to continue the day, Larry drove straight home. He settled down for some shut-eye on his cozy unmade bed. A couple of hours later, the telephone rang. Since Jerry was home, he answered it. The caller spoke with a British accent and asked to talk to Larry, so Jerry told him to hold on so he could get Larry from his bedroom. "Larry, get up! There's a caller on the phone with a British accent." Larry scrambled to his feet with excitement and scurried over to where Jerry left the telephone. Larry thought Brian's accent was so cool. Brian asked Larry, "What are you doing this evening?" Larry replied, "I have to work

2. Pandora's Box was located at 8118 Sunset Blvd. on an island of land at Crescent Heights Blvd. It is where the famous 'Sunset Strip Curfew Riots' started when teenage tensions boiled over. Jimmy O'Neill was host of the popular dance show called 'Shindig' and also the owner of Pandora's Box.

driving a cab tonight until 11:00 P.M. He added that he would call him at his bungalow if he finished work earlier. Neither could have guessed how many more get together opportunities would follow.

About thirty minutes had passed since the telephone call from Brian. With a jolt of thought, Larry decided he would not go to work that day. "Why not, this was a special occasion! The taxi job can wait ... it'll be there tomorrow." He called the Yellow Cab Company and said he wouldn't be going in that evening due to an emergency, (one he made up spur of the moment.) After he hung up, the next call he made was to Brian at his bungalow. Thankfully, Brian answered. Larry told him about the change of work plans in favor of getting together with him for the evening. Brian was excited to hear they could get together earlier than initially planned and happy he didn't make other plans.

Brian told him to drive over to his bungalow around 6:00 P.M. so they could go out somewhere to eat. He was aware of the fact that Larry knew Hollywood better than most, and with so many great restaurants to choose from he was in a better position to suggest the right place to have supper. Brian also told Larry not to worry about money; he would cover all costs for dinner that evening. Feeling embarrassed, he gave the offer some thought but then was relieved and grateful since his finances were low.

Larry put considerable thought into what to wear, wanting to put his best look forward. Since the evening weather was cooler, he decided to wear a nice pair of brown dress slacks with a soft yellow 'v' neck alpaca sweater. A pair of dark brown leather penny loafers completed that selection. He wanted to give his best impression to Brian and show him he knew how to dress well.

Rushing to get his car in the garage, Larry skipped down the stairs and put the key in the ignition. He put the key into the ignition, but his shabby little Fiat didn't start. Larry got out, gave the car a hard fast push, jumped back in, and popped the clutch. With a bang, the engine cranked over and started. Larry thought, "A guy and his car always have a special relationship."

CHAPTER NINE

THE CONFESSION

It was a glorious summer evening in Southern California. Palm trees waved slightly in the gentle winds that came off the Pacific Ocean, traveling west towards Los Angeles, into the Hills of Beverly. Larry cruised along Sunset Boulevard before making a hard right-hand turn on North Crescent Drive. He continued heading north for about 50 yards before hanging a U-turn after he saw a parking space near the front of Bungalow 6A.

Brian anticipated Larry's arrival and met him outside the bungalow. Brian walked over to him and jumped into the car. "Hello Larry," said Brian in his cool British accent. "It's so good to see you again so soon. I don't have many opportunities to be so casual about going out to eat or do anything that doesn't have a spotlight on it. This is so refreshing." After an intimate but friendly hug, Larry recommended they drive to La

Rue Restaurant.[1] It was a popular eating spot located on Sunset Blvd. and Sunset Plaza Drive. Being a weekend night was risky, but because it was early, Larry felt confident that there would be fewer looky-loos and that Brian would feel comfortable at the  restaurant. Also, they should be able to get a table without reservations. He told Brian to let him know if he felt any discomfort with the place, the people, or the atmosphere, and they would leave immediately. Larry also reminded Brian he knew many wonderful places to dine.

As Larry pulled up to the front of the restaurant, the valet attendants rushed over to the car, showing excellent customer service, and opened both car doors to greet them. Larry agreed to let the valet park his vehicle with the understanding that he would need to get the car himself when

---

1. La Rue Restaurant opened in 1944. It was located 8361 Sunset Blvd and was in operation until 1969. The interior décor was lush and rich with pistachio and coca striped booths. Guests would wait for a table while sitting at red leather can ebony bar. Bill Wilkerson was the owner; he also owned *The Hollywood Reporter* and famous nightclubs such as Ciros's, Café Trachadero and the famous Flamingo Hotel in Las Vegas

they were ready to leave. The valet attendant agreed, and Larry gave him a generous tip before they headed for the front door of La Rues. Brian looked questionably at Larry when he tipped the attendant and asked, "Why did you tip him for parking the car?" Larry replied, "In America, tipping is what makes the world go round. People live off of their tips; it's customary." Brian nodded and replied," Oh, got it. I'll have to get used to these non-British customs."

Once they walked inside the restaurant, Brian immediately felt uncomfortable with how crowded the restaurant was. Brian didn't care for the crowds, even though he had no choice at certain times. He couldn't relax with people staring at him. For some reason that night it seemed all eyes were on him as he walked through the door. Besides, Brian felt he was underdressed. After expressing his anxiety to Larry, they agreed to find somewhere else to eat. They walked out of the restaurant, and Larry retrieved his keys from the valet. Then both walked towards the back of the restaurant to the parking lot and found the car.

Larry jumped into the driver's seat and asked Brian if he would mind giving the car a push if it didn't start. Brian's reply was, "Pardon me, did you say for me to push the car? Larry turned the key in the ignition to show Brian it wouldn't start. Brian chuckled and said, "At your service, my good man!" He wasn't sure what to expect but went behind the car as directed so he could push while Larry worked the clutch and got it started. Brian chuckled and hopped into the passenger seat. Turning to Larry, he said, "I've never done that before. That was great fun! Brilliant! And off they drove into the night in search of a good meal and a good time.

Larry decided to take Brian to Dresden's, located across town in East Hollywood in the Los Feliz area. Larry took the scenic route down Sunset. Arriving at the intersection of Vine and Sunset, he made a left on Vine Street. Pointing out the famous Wallich's Music City.[2] Larry mentioned that it was

2. Wallich's Music City was the premier record store in Southern California and the largest specialty record store in Los Angeles, located on Sunset and Vine at 1555 Vine Street in Hollywood

the most popular music store in Hollywood. He told Brian that inside Wallich's Music store, customers could play records in private listening booths. Music lovers young and old would hang out in the booths, listening to music, whether they were planning to buy or not. Brian mentioned they have the same type of listening booths inside NEMS[3] in Liverpool,

England. Brian went on to explain NEMS is short for North End Music Stores and owned by his family. He told Larry he managed the record department before becoming involved with managing the Beatles.

They continued to drive north on Vine Street and passed the famous Brown Derby Restaurant.[4] Larry pointed out that according to local legend; the Brown Derby invented the Cobb Salad. Larry gunned the engine as they passed the Capitol Records building.[5]

90028. Glenn E. Wallichs, and his brother Clyde owned the record store opening in 1940 and closed in 1978. Glenn also started Capitol Records along with Savannah Georgia born songwriter Johnny Mercer, and ex-Paramount Producer Buddy De Silva.

3. NEMS started as a family owned furniture store that also sold musical instruments and vinyl records. NEMS stands for 'North End Music Stores'. Brian Epstein joined his family business in the late 1950s as manager of the record department when the new store opened in Liverpool. This is where Brian first met up with John Lennon.

4. The Brown Derby -was the name of a chain of restaurants in Los Angeles, California. The first and most famous of these was shaped like a man's derby hat, an iconic image that became synonymous with the Golden Age of Hollywood. The original restaurant was located at 3427 Wilshire Boulevard and opened in 1926. The restaurants started by Robert H. Cobb created the famous Cobb Salad. The second Brown Derby with a Spanish Mission style façade, opened on Valentine's Day in 1929 at 1628 North Vine Street in Hollywood.

5. The Capitol Records Tower is a thirteen-story circular office-building tower located at 1750 Vine Street, Hollywood, CA 90028; designed by twenty four year old Louis Naidorf. It was built to resemble a stack of records on a turntable. The blinking red light atop of the tower, blinking at night, spells out the name of "Hollywood" in Morse code. This was an idea of then President of Capitol Records, Alan Livingston. Glenn E. Wallichs, Johnny Mercer, and Buddy De Silva owned

The building was famous for its innovative architecture; it looked a stack of towering records with a needle on top. "Capitol Records has recently become home for the Beatles recording label in the United States," commented Brian, "so I'll probably be spending a lot of time there when in Los Angeles."

As they came around the bend on Los Feliz, Larry pointed out Griffith Park,[6] the largest urban park in North America. Larry told Brian to look further up into the hills to the left to see the Griffith Park Observatory; a fabulous art deco building that commanded a view on the slope of Mount Hollywood. In 1955, the movie *Rebel Without A Cause* was filmed at the Observatory. The stars of that movie were James Dean, Natalie Wood, and Sal Mineo.[7] Brian told Larry that he was friends with Sal Mineo, and one day he would introduce him to Sal.

Reaching their destination, Larry parked behind Dresden Restaurant.[8] Larry asked Brian, "Do you think I would make a good tour guide?" Brian responded, "Well, I would never have come to know all this wonderful information if it wasn't for you. Thank you, Larry!" Brian continued, "As a child, I dreamed about Hollywood, the movie stars, and their beautiful homes. Now, I'm here, in the city of dreams, and Hollywood has opened up its arms to me. It may seem odd to you because you were born here, but it's a dream come true for me."

As they moved closer towards the entrance, Brian said, "I remember my mother smoking an English brand of what in colloquial British terms are called Fags, the Player Medium Navy Cut brand of cigarettes." The name was an acronym used during WWII for "For a Good Smoke." Brian loved collecting the inserted cards of movie stars and musicians they packaged

Capitol Records. The building exists in the same location as of 2019.

6. Griffith Park was donated by *Griffith J. Griffith, a Welsh businessman and philanthropist. After accumulating a significant fortune from a mining syndicate in the 1880's Griffith donated 3015 acres to the City of Los Angeles, which became known as Griffith Park. Unfortunately, Griffith was arrested for the attempted murder of his wife, which is what he became known for the most. The shooting of his wife in 1903, a crime that he only served for two years in prison, marred his legacy forever. The park is still open and used by locals and tourists from all over the world. Griffith died in Los Angeles in1909 at the age of 69.

7. Sal Mineo was born Salvatore Mineo, Jr. (January 10, 1939-February 12, 1976), and was an American film and theatre actor known for his performance of as "Plato" in the movie *Rebel Without A Cause* staring opposite James Dean. He was nominated twice for an Academy Award for Best Supporting Actor for his roles in *Rebel Without A Cause*(1955) and *Exodus* (1960).

8. The Dresden Restaurant is still located at 1760 Vermont Ave in Los Angeles California 90027

inside. My mother shared her cards with me, and I collected them for a while, but honestly, I was only interested in the cards with movie stars, especially the stars from Hollywood." As they walked towards the back door entrance, Larry opened the door, and they both walked into Dresden.

The place looked beautiful inside, with dim lighting and soft white leather booths. "First impression is a good one," said Brian as he gestured a thumbs up with his hand. The maître d' escorted them both to a lovely table with high back white leather chairs fit for a King.

It was a perfect place for them to have a quiet and intimate evening. As soon as they sat down, Larry spoke up about his curiosity about where Brian was currently living in England. Brian said he lived in a beautiful two-bedroom apartment in Whaddon House on William Mews in Knightsbridge, a small private street near Harrods. Larry never heard of the word "Mews" and asked Brian to explain. Brian went on to share that it's primarily a British term describing a row of stables, usually with carriage houses below and living quarters above converted to modern dwellings. Brian said he was thinking about moving to another place, one that was a little more spacious, and he hoped to find a new home soon.

They took a breather from the conversation so that Brian could order a bottle of good French wine. After approving the wine, they raised their glasses and toasted the evening. Brian's choice of wine was perfect! They had a delightful time toasting to just about anything, for any good reason. Brian continued to open up even more and revealed secrets about his private life in England.

Brian was born in a middle-class neighborhood in England, but his upbringing was strictly upper class. His parents taught him good manners and behavior. Brian was a rather shy and proper acting man. I guess you would say a very British man. Brian elaborated with more details about his parents. In the early 1950s, they owned a furniture store in Liverpool that became a music store named NEMS. Brian's father's name was Harry, and his mummy's name was Malka, known as Queenie. Brian adored his parents, but even more so, his mum Queenie, as she was a very loving and understanding mother. Queenie was even more special to him after she lovingly accepted Brian's sexual preferences. He could talk to her about anything and everything.

In a touching moment, Brian stumbled for words and became quiet. Here was a man on top of the world, yet in many ways, feeling left behind Larry gently asked him if he was okay. With a sad look, Brian said, "I love the boys, my lads, but I am not one of the boys. Even though I am a part of it and certainly guiding their ship, I feel like I have no one to share my conquests, no one to love, and no one that loves me back. You know what I'm talking about, a genuinely heartfelt and true love!" Brian choked up as he spoke and started to shed a tear. He didn't completely let go because he was in a public place. Brian always tried to have a stiff upper lip about things. He revealed to Larry how important having a friendship with him was. There was a moment of silence as they looked into each other's eyes.

It was a heartfelt moment. Brian added that he hoped and prayed Larry understood and would never betray him. Larry looked Brian straight in the eyes and said, "I would never betray you or the friendship we have, never, that is a promise I make to you now." At that very moment, comforting warmth set in. Trust grew between them. Something extraordinary was happening, and it pulled them together like a magnet.

For Brian, it just might be the kind of relationship he had always dreamed of having. For Larry, it was like catching lightning in a bottle, and in reality, he hoped it would result in having a lifelong friend. Larry remembered how tender that moment was, and to this day will never forget it as long as he lives.

Brian continued, saying he had a difficult time in school because he was more interested in theater life, and had even considered fashion design. He told Larry about his short-lived army experience and how he was able to get out of the army without serving a full term. Larry said that he too was in the military, the Air Force to be exact, and served four years. After the military, Brian's father thought Brian might do well running the record department branch of NEMS. Brian liked that idea and took that job seriously. He had an ear for music and felt he knew what type of music various age groups would enjoy.

They finished dinner, Brian paid the bill, and both walked out, slowly heading towards the car. Brian suggested they take a little walk in the neighborhood first before driving to allow some of the wine effect to wear off. Larry agreed, so they walked down Vermont Avenue, leaving the car in Dresden's parking lot. Somehow, with so many people in the world to compare with, they shared many of the same emotional connections and same problems with life while dealing with the struggles of being gay. It seemed to be a match made in heaven.

CHAPTER TEN

THE BULL FIGHTER AND ZSA ZSA GABOR

When Brian traveled to Los Angeles, he always stayed at the Beverly Hills Hotel bungalow. Larry assisted Brian with a variety of administrative tasks during the day, which then allowed for more time spent together. With business done for the day, they enjoyed just having fun. Tasks assigned included answering the phone, taking down notes as Brian came up with ideas, providing delivery assistance, and organizing his schedule and calendar. Larry made sure that Brian's personal and business calendars did not conflict.

The amount of time he was spending with Brian eventually led to Larry not being available to drive a taxicab. They continued to have great fun, along with dining in many diverse restaurants. There was an allotment of time spent in having cocktails within the safety of dimly lit clubs in Hollywood. Those bars and clubs included a hidden gay underworld where they could share some much needed time relaxing together. Larry always felt Brian had a difficult time relaxing.

Because Brian had a large number of business details to attend to when in Los Angeles, he asked Larry to continue helping him as much as possible. The idea was for him to perform as his California assistant, off the books. In actuality, Brian was trying to keep Larry busy with his business so he could stay closer to him. Since Larry was very much into the music business and the type of nightlife it created, he looked forward to the task and was excited to help in any way he could. It was a better job than driving a taxi! Just being around, Brian made for great fun and personal adventure. Larry often thought it was a dream being able to assist such a powerful man and mentor in the music business, especially how he was helping a man he had grown to care for so deeply.

When at the Beverly Hills Hotel, they would find time to sit on the patio chairs outside the door of the bungalow and enjoy the warm and lovely California nights. Brian seemed to relax during those rare moments and always shared stories with Larry. They were always sharing life stories about friends, family, country, business, or sexual escapades.

One of Brian's most treasured stories was his love of bullfighting. Brian expressed himself eloquently by saying, "The bullfight is truly life's theater where someone or something will perish." Brian saw the art in the bullfight, the pageantry, not the blood or torture. He had a passionate admiration for the world-famous matador El Cordobes. In Spain, he was known as "the Spanish Beatle" because of his boyish good looks and his Beatle style hair. The bullfighter's real name was Manuel Benitez Perez. To his friends he was called "Manolito." Inside the bathroom and on the wall of Brian's new home was an eight-foot tall photo of El Cordobes' face. Brian was smitten with the boyish Manolito.

Brian told Larry he would have loved to manage El Cordobes and gave it a lot of effort in trying to do so. Brian wanted to get him into the movie business because he was so handsome and appealing to the eye. Manolito's manager's name was Pipo and Brian with Geoffrey Ellis went to visit El Cordobes at his ranch in Cordoba. Brian talked with Pipo about having El Cordobes in the Beatles next movie, but Pipo would not hear of it saying that the brave El Cordobes wasn't interested in that kind of fame. It became apparent to Larry that Brian would have El Cordobes as his lover if given the opportunity. Larry could see the sexual excitement in Brian's eyes and flushed skin. Sadly all he could do was fantasize about that possibility.

On one of Brian's trips to Spain, he invited Beatle John to join him. John's wife, Cynthia, had just given birth to their first child, and John was in no mood to hang around and help with the baby. Back in Liverpool, rumors were rampant that John and Brian had a sexual relationship. "What happened," John explained, "is that Eppy just kept on and on at me. Until one night, I finally just pulled me trousers down and said to him: 'Oh, for Christ's sake, Brian, just stick it up me fucking arse then.'

"And he said to me, 'Actually, John, I don't do that kind of thing. That's not what I like to do. Well,' I said, 'what is it you like to do, then?'"

"And he said, 'I'd really just like to touch you, John.'"

"And so I let him toss me off."

And that was that. End of story.

Brian also told Larry the reason he put the Beatles in suits. His reasoning was so the parents of teenagers would like them too. Brian thought a "clean" wholesome classy look for the Beatles would work much better for their image than the leather jackets and jeans they were used to wearing when he first met them at the Cavern. He was so right.

They were about to leave the bungalow after having considered a drive to the beach when the telephone rang. Larry jumped to answer the phone only to find out the caller was the famous actress Zsa Zsa Gabor[1] on the

---

1. Zsa Zsa Gabor was born Sari Gabor on February 6th 1917 and died December 18, 2016. She was a

other end of the receiver. Instantly Larry recognized that voice with the Hungarian accent. "Well, hello Zsa Zsa, how can I be of service?" He spoke in a tone of being very proper and polite. After that brief phone salutation, Larry informed her that he was answering Brian's calls. She asked to speak with Brian if he was available. Off to the side of Larry's peripheral vision, he saw that Brian motioned a wave-her-off when he heard the name. He pleaded with Larry by gestures, going down on his knees in the most comical way, with the use of hand gestures like a mime to suggest he would rather slit his throat than talk with her. He begged Larry to get rid of her. It was hard for Larry not to fall over with laughter. Here he was talking with Zsa Zsa with her "Dahling" this and "Dahling" that, and Brian on his knees begging for him to hang up the phone.

Larry removed his hand from covering up the phone receiver and said in a stern but polite voice, "I'm sorry, but Mr. Epstein isn't available to talk right now." Zsa Zsa asked Larry to relay a message that she was having a dinner party at her home in Beverly Hills, and she wanted him to attend. Larry agreed to pass along the message and hung up the phone. He realized that she neglected to mention the date and time. Oh well! Brian was still down on the carpet when he stopped to say he didn't want to attend her party to be put on a pedestal as being one of the closest persons to the Beatles. There was a bit of disgust along with a tinge of anger behind Brian's laughter that stung Larry's memory forever. He hadn't heard Brian talk that way before.

About an hour later, they were still at the bungalow, when there was an unexpected knock at the door. Larry walked over to answer it. Standing on the other side of the door was a pretty young girl who identified herself as Zsa Zsa's daughter, Francesca Hilton. Larry was surprised that Zsa Zsa sent her daughter to deliver a personal invitation to her mother's dinner party. So Larry told Francesca that he would pass along the message to Brian. He also volunteered that he didn't think Mr. Epstein would have the time to attend due to his busy schedule. Then he extended a sincere apology and a thank you to be expressed to Zsa Zsa. From that moment on, as it turned out, Larry was the instigator of pranks whenever it came to Zsa Zsa Gabor. Larry remembers that Brian loved every minute of it.

Larry was surprised that Brian had that type of humor in him. He wanted Larry to keep that woman away no matter what he had to do. Brian wasn't sure about what her intentions or ulterior motives might have

Hungarian-American actress and socialite. She had three sisters. She was known for her extravagant Hollywood driven lifestyle. She was married to nine husbands, including hotel magnate Conrad Hilton and actor George Sanders.

been. And, if she was just interested in adding him to her list of younger men that she seduced, that was never going to happen! However, Zsa Zsa was relentless with her telephone calls to the bungalow, saying each time she wanted to make sure that Brian received her messages.

Larry randomly took on various accents when answering those calls from Zsa Zsa, pretending there were multiple levels of people she had to go through before speaking with Brian. She became more irritated and flustered each time and would just hang up the phone. Another time when he answered one of Zsa Zsa's calls, Larry created a character with a hair lip, which was cruel but incredibly hysterical.

One evening Brian called Larry and asked him to be his guest at La Scala Restaurant[2] in Beverly Hills. Larry was surprised by that request because he thought Brian wouldn't like La Scala due to the number of celebrities and paparazzi. But Brian wanted to impress a couple of his  good friends, and he was willing to deal with the extra attention and Beverly Hills hoopla. Those friends were Lionel Bart, who was visiting Los Angeles at the time and Sal Mineo, who was in between making movies. Loving that responsibility, Larry drove by the hotel bungalow to pick up Brian. They wouldn't have far to drive to the restaurant. Within minutes after picking Brian up, they arrived at La Scala.

Entering "Jean Leon's La Scala," it was immediately apparent the room was full of prominent and high-status people. No eyes turned towards them, as everyone there was someone of importance. Having decided they would make the evening a memorable one, they dressed to impress. Brian wore a dark gray Italian suit with matching vest, a crisp white button-down collared shirt, and a black-toned paisley tie. Larry wore a black sharkskin suit, a white dress shirt with gold cuff links, and a black striped skinny tie. Needless to say, they looked very sharp.

And as luck would have it, straight ahead in front of them was Zsa Zsa. She walked around; being the charming and beautiful socialite that she was. The waiter greeted them and showed them to a booth directly across from none other than Zsa Zsa. With those seating arrangements, fun for the evening was sure to follow. Lionel arrived

2. La Scala Restaurant is located at 434 Canon Dr. Beverly Hills, CA 90210. The original La Scala was located on Little Santa Monica Blvd.

shortly afterward, as did Sal. Brian introduced Larry to Sal then quickly briefed his friends on the frequent phone calls from Zsa Zsa. He laughed out loud when providing details about the pranks Larry pulled on her.

Lionel urged Larry on about starting a conversation with Zsa Zsa. But before that happened, Zsa Zsa stood up and extended her hand out to everyone at Brian's booth, saying, "Hello Dahlings." She desperately tried to engage a conversation with anyone at the table, but they were not yet ready and gave the impression of being distracted while looking at the menu. Lionel turned his back on Zsa Zsa, pretending to cough, and started making faces while crossing his eyes at Brian just out of eyesight of Zsa Zsa. That gave Larry a window of opportunity to jump in and start fooling around in banter conversation with Zsa Zsa. But she returned to her booth to rejoin her guests and continue eating. Lionel turned closer to Brian and Larry and whispered in the most upper-class British accent, "You know Brian; I believe the dear lady wants to suck your cock! And if not, I am sure she would love to put her nails into Larry's back!" They all roared with laughter, causing everyone seated in the area to turn heads in their direction.

Zsa Zsa stood up again, and moving closer to Larry told him that Brian hired a horrible person that was answering his phone calls. Larry just laughed because she was talking about him. Larry tried hard to keep a straight face, but as if being challenged returned some rather choice and brash words to her. Zsa Zsa looked stunned for a moment but then realized the person she had talked to all those times was now the person sitting in front of her. After turning various shades of purple, she turned away and sat down. Further communication between them stopped after she returned to her table. As Zsa Zsa was leaving, she walked directly over to Brian's booth and greeted them all a farewell and a good evening. You had to take notice of that woman; she had class like no other; that wonderful Zsa Zsa Gabor.

It wasn't long before another party invitation for Brian to attend was received, and that one required an RSVP. It was difficult to believe that Zsa Zsa had made another attempt and request for Brian to attend one of her parties. Zsa Zsa was certainly intent with making Brian a part of her life. Brian gave it some thought and responded that he and a guest would attend. That guest turned out to be Larry. Surprised by Brian's acceptance, he happily went along with it. They both thought it would be another opportunity for more sadistic fun, once again, at Zsa Zsa's expense. Instead, they would attempt to be perfect gentlemen.

Zsa Zsa's party was at a nightclub called the Crescendo,[3] located on the Sunset Strip. The Crescendo was a well-known hot spot featuring a lot of great jazz and blues artists. Brian hired a limo so Larry wouldn't need to drive. They arrived at the party on time and as usual, were dressed to

the nines. Larry was wearing the same suit he wore to La Scala. Zsa Zsa wore a low cut pink satin dress. She was in top form displaying her charismatic and infectious personality, signature bold lips, and her sex appeal.

Zsa Zsa rented the entire 2nd floor of the Crescendo for her party guests, and she invited the "Who's Who" of Hollywood to the party so everyone could meet Brian Epstein. Johnny Grant, an actor and radio personality along with Paramount's young executive producer A.C. Lyles and many others of that caliber, were in attendance. Just about anyone important in Hollywood was there, and by all definitions, this was very much a classic "Hollywood" Party. Larry and Brian behaved, and only made fun of her under wraps. It turned out to be a rather lovely evening for everyone. And yes, Zsa Zsa won them over with her magical appeal. The party was a success for Zsa Zsa and set a very positive image with Brian for the future.

Deciding to do something different one lazy afternoon, they went out to a popular club called the Red Raven,[4] on Melrose Avenue. It was an underground gay club in Hollywood, now known as West Hollywood. When the drinks arrived, they toasted to a blossoming friendship. After a bit of light conversation, Larry explained that just before he graduated from high school, he and a friend named Dickie Hall went into business together at a gas station. The owner of the station was going through hard times and he allowed the two boys to run the place. Interestingly enough, Dickie Hall had been a child actor in Hollywood staring in many of the early "Our Gang" comedies. That period was the worst part of Dickies' life. One would think that a child actor would have an advantage over other up and coming actors but this wasn't the case. Shortly after "Our Gang" ended, both of his parents committed suicide! Brian commented

---

3. Crescendo was located at 8572 Sunset Blvd, Sunset Strip. It was open in 1954 and closed in 1964. It was a music jazz and comedy venue. Gene Norman owned the Crescendo. He also owned GNP Crescendo Records. It was located right next to the Playboy Club.
4. Red Raven Cocktail Lounge was located on 7013 Melrose Ave, Hollywood 90038. It's now an Indian Restaurant called Anarkali.

that Hollywood could be as hard a place as anywhere in the world. Life was good and there was no indication how hard life was going to get.

One afternoon when Larry was relaxing at his apartment having a beer with Jerry, Diz Gillespie dropped by unexpectedly for a visit. Shortly after his arrival, the telephone rang, so Larry jumped up to answer it. A male caller with a lovely French accent was on the phone, and he said, "This is Alain Delon[5] calling for Larry Stanton." Larry was amazed when he heard that voice and accent, but smiled as he realized who it was and who was responsible for that call coming in. Larry responded with an amicable tone and said, "Hello," thanked him for calling, and then said, "I think my roommate would love to talk with you. Hold on just one moment, and let me put Jerry on the phone with you." Then he quickly passed the phone over to Jerry without identifying who it was, so there would be an element of surprise. They had a pleasant conversation that lasted for about ten minutes, and Larry could see Jerry's blushing face just before he hung up the telephone. Larry explained to Jerry how Alain just happened to call informing them that Brian was responsible. Larry couldn't wait to thank Brian for the surprise telephone call he had arranged and how delightful it was for thinking about it. Sitting in the corner of the room was Diz, who was intensely observing and taking it all in. Larry recalled he could almost see the wheels turning in Diz's head. He was up to something, but just what remained unknown?

5. Alain Fabien Maurice Marcel Delon known to the cinema world as Alan Delon. He is French born on November 8th in 1935. He became one of Europe's important actors and sex symbols in the 1960's. Delon eventually decided to obtain Swiss citizenship on 9/23/99 and currently lives in Chene-Bourgeries in Geneva.

CHAPTER ELEVEN

LARRY SURVIVES DIZ (LSD) NAKED IN THE HOLLYWOOD HILLS

B rian decided he would throw another party at the Beverly Hills Hotel bungalow and just invited a select group of people he liked. Being it was a smaller party made it easier for everyone to see when and who showed up. Larry had been with Brian all day and therefore acted as co-host with Brian when greeting guests as they arrived. To Larry's surprise and Brian's excitement, Diz Gillespie made an appearance. Brian sent a special invitation by way of a phone call to Jerry for Diz to attend the party. It seemed odd to Larry that Brian snuck that invite in without his knowledge. The party rolled out slow and easy, drinks were poured, pills were popped, joints were smoked, and someone had very suspiciously laced a few drinks with LSD. Of course, that wasn't known until much later on during the party.

Diz surprised Larry by way of a very kind gesture and brought a drink over to him. Larry thanked him and thought he was acting suspiciously nice. If Larry was about to indulge in another night of drinking and marijuana, he wanted to make sure his stomach was filled with enough food so he wouldn't get sick or become too high.

As the party progressed into the evening hours, the music volume became louder. In the background, Brian's guests paired up and looked to get cozier in the hallways and bathrooms. In just about every nook and cranny of the bungalow, you could see potential lovers looking to have a good time and sexual fun. Some party attendees started to show signs of affection towards their partner of choice, openly groping and kissing for all eyes to see. There were sounds of sexual lust behind the bathroom door. Those sounds filled the party atmosphere with heavy sighs and moans of ecstasy. "Hey, just what kind of party is this?" Larry said softly so no one else would hear. In another bathroom came sounds as if someone was snorting their brains out. It was strange to hear cocaine being snorted that way, and it came out of the bathroom with an echo of surround sound.

The bathroom doors opened frequently, and couples would switch places anxious to do some drugs behind closed doors. Other couples used the bathrooms for fucking, blowjobs, and whatever else turned them on. Some couples couldn't wait. The party had turned into one wild orgy. It began to appear out of control with all the sex, drugs, and Rock n' Roll music in the room. The entire bungalow took on the penetrating odor of the devil's lettuce. Did Brian realize this would happen? Larry sat there watching and wondering as he began to feel what he thought was a contact high from it all.

At one point during the evening, Brian realized Larry was nowhere to be found. He seemed to be missing in action, and Brian quickly became concerned. Brian had been preoccupied in conversations with three other young men, but one of them had hijacked Brian's complete attention. That young man was Diz Gillespie. Diz had intentionally occupied all of Brian's attention.

It was unlike Larry to walk away or leave without informing Brian or anyone as to where he was going. Brian stopped talking with Diz and briskly walked out to the patio to ask if anyone had recently seen Larry. One guy who was completely loaded turned to Brian and said, "Yes, I saw him. He left about an hour ago, and you know what, he was walking around stark naked and seemed to be out of his head. I saw him run out the front door. I'm sorry, but we all just stood around and watched. We should have reacted and stopped him."

It was hard for Brian to digest the thought of something terrible or crazy happening to Larry, but he also couldn't help noticing how the party had gotten out of control. Fueled by drugs, lust, music, and sex, it had turned into an orgy of hedonistic pleasure. Diz approached Brian and asked in a cunning voice, "You look, upset man, what are you upset about?" Brian replied, "I'm worried about Larry. No one has seen him for an hour or so, and I heard he is out there somewhere running around without his clothes. That isn't like Larry at all." Diz then said, "Oh well, he must be having a bad trip. I spiked his drink with LSD. I wanted some folks to try the stuff, so he's probably out there just tripping Brian, I'm sure he'll be fine." Immediately Brian became even more upset and told Diz to step aside and not bother him. He quickly decided the most prudent thing would be to call the Beverly Hills Police Department. He wouldn't take the chance that something terrible could happen to Larry, or even hear there had been an accident. It could all end up printed in some scandalous news article at Larry's expense. Larry was too important to him; he had to find out where he was.

He stood in the middle of the living room and yelled out loud that he would be calling the police. Before he could finish saying the word police, everyone scattered gathering their belongings and then quickly left the party. Right before he called the cops, Brian walked around all rooms and cleaned up the litter of drugs and paraphernalia. He opened up all the windows and put the air conditioning on to help blow out all the marijuana smoke that filled the air inside the bungalow. Once that was done, Brian called the Beverly Hills Police Department. Brian needed the situation to be handled with great delicacy and without attracting any hotel management, press, or publicity.

Usually paparazzi were close by due to the high profile of celebrity visitors at the hotel. So he wanted to be careful.

When the police arrived, he asked them to be careful and discreet when they located Larry. As a favor, he asked that Larry be brought back to his bungalow, telling the police he would take full responsibility and care of him.

Brian used his celebrity status to get the police to work with him without the situation being blown out of proportion. Thank God, the police officers that showed up at the bungalow were Beatles fans. To win them over, Brian gave each police officer a couple of Beatle records along with an autographed photo of Cilla Black. On all accounts, Brian's ability to charm and persuade had worked. The police officers assured Brian that everything would work out as he wished. Then they left the bungalow to search for Larry. The police searched the entire area of the hotel, searched the park across the street as well as the foothills. They extended their perimeters and searched in every direction.

The police finally located Larry, walking around in the hills stark naked. Larry wasn't combative when the police approached, but he was utterly embarrassed. He had no idea where he was or how he got there and was still high, slowly coming back to reality. Larry profusely apologized to the officers for having to track him down. He was ashamed to be exposing his all in his birthday suit. The police assisted Larry into the back seat of their car and gave him a blanket, which he wrapped around his body. As the police car got closer to the hotel, all Larry could think about was what Brian would think. That was a good sign; the drugs were starting to wear off. It was apparent to the police that Larry had experienced a bad drug trip. They helped Brian Epstein and did him a big favor due to his prestige, and their love of Beatle music.

When the police arrived at Brian's bungalow with Larry in tow, Brian thanked the officers for taking care of Larry and for being so compassionate and understanding. He could have been arrested for indecent exposure and for being under the influence. Brian quickly put Larry to bed, tucked him in nicely, and told him to stay in bed while he made a cup of tea for them both. Brian was protecting and caring for Larry just as a mother would do for her child. Diz left with the other guests, sneaking out without so much as an apology for traumatizing Larry and ruining Brian's party. When Larry felt better, Brian told him all the details that led up to his being found naked and alone in the darkness of Beverly Hills. For Brian to call the police was an enormous act of trust; Brian had not always gotten on well with the police.

One night in 1959, when Brian was just 25 years old, he parked his car down the street from a public bathroom. He waited in his car, shielded from view by the dark moonless sky until after a long time he spotted a man walking towards the bathroom. The man was bigger and older than Brian, and after stopping for a moment, the man went inside the dingy dimly lit men's room. Brian immediately got up out of his car, locked it, and hurriedly followed the man in.

Once inside, Brian solicited the man, and instead of retiring into one of the unoccupied stalls, the man beat Brian severely and mercilessly, leaving him lying on the wet floor. The man had stolen Brian's watch, his wallet and his money. Upon regaining his wits, he ran sobbing to his car and drove frantically to his parent's home in Childwell. That wasn't the end of the story. While Brian was crying and recounting the events to Queenie, the phone rang; it was the man who had just assaulted Brian. He had recognized Brian's name as one of a prominent well to do family, and he wanted money to keep silent about Brian's solicitations.

Queenie called the police, who asked Brian to set a trap for the blackmailer. He was to agree to pay whatever the man wanted and set up a place to meet the man. On the following night, Brian waited for the man on a dark corner in Whitechapel, and at the appointed time, he appeared from across the street. As soon as the man demanded the money, Brian gave a pre-arranged signal, and the police pounced. The ensuing court trial nearly destroyed Brian, who was ordered to see a psychiatrist.

CHAPTER TWELVE

THREE IN A JACUZZI

A few more days passed, and the craziness from the wild party at Brian's had quieted down. Larry felt a bit more recovered from that traumatic LSD experience. Other partygoers forgot about the drama, and it was written off as another wild Hollywood secret event.

Brian and Larry looked forward to a quiet and enjoyable evening on their next rendezvous. On that particular get-together, Larry accompanied Brian on a visit to actor Laurence Harvey's[1] house above the Beverly Hills Hotel. Laurence Harvey would not be at home during their stay, but the three beautifully designed buildings at the top were lit and offered a dramatic welcome. The main house sat on three acres and was built in 1963 by Architectural Designers Buff and Hensman[2] specifically for Laurence Harvey. The extravagant property had a private security service that ensured privacy and protection. Brian shared that he visited Harvey's guesthouse a couple of times when indulging in sexual escapades with a few young men. Larry felt a tinge of jealousy but quickly stopped himself from thinking those kinds of thoughts. He didn't want their relationship tangled in that type of web. Brian loved the place for its incredible view and outside colors of light purple and brilliant red. He considered buying the property from Laurence and making it his home in California. He was also looking for a house the Beatles could stay in when in Los Angeles.

Along with Larry and Brian, was Lionel Bart. Laurence arranged for one of his trusted security guards to be there, allowing Brian and his guests open access to the house and surrounding area. Adding a special touch to the evening, Lionel brought along a couple of bottles of expensive wine and three crystal long stem glasses. Finally able to relax, the three men sat

1. Laurence Harvey once lived at 1196 Cabrillo Dr. in Beverly Hills California 90210. He was British actor with looks similar to a current actor of today, Jude Law. There have been many stories about Mr. Harvey; one of them is that he was never without a cigarette and drink in his hand. He was born Zvi Mosheh Skikne in 1928 in Lithuania, and born of Jewish faith. It's rumored that his sexuality was not really defined and often thought of as being homosexual, but he kept this as private as one could and married a woman in order to keep his image as a matinee idle intact. He was married a few times; on the last marriage he finally had a daughter and felt blessed to have her in his life. He died on November 25th 1973 in Hampstead, England.
2. Buff and Hensman was a Southern California Architectural firm. It seems that the post war dream between 1950 and 2000 helped define this firm. They used the slogan "Build California Dreams" in their marketing and their timeless designs have lasted for over fifty years.

in the Jacuzzi soaking in the warm bubbling water and marveling at the swath of bright shining stars set against the dark L.A. sky. It was a fabulous view. Lionel opened one of the bottles of wine and poured each one of them a glass. The three friends raised their glasses and toasted their good fortune.

Even in this state of relaxation, Brian was thinking about his Beatles. The Beatles wanted to meet their idol, Elvis Presley. He knew that Elvis leased a house in Beverly Hills, so he asked Larry to make a mental note and assist in making that meeting happen. Any meeting would have to be arranged through Elvis's manager Colonel Tom Parker. That would be no easy task. Lionel quipped in a dry British tone while flamboyantly waving his arms in the air, "You can make anything happen, Brian, you are the newest king here in Hollywood, so enjoy it all while you can, my dear Brian." They laughed, raised their glasses for another toast, and took more sips of the delightful wine they were happily indulging in.

After finishing their first bottle of wine, Brian decided it was time to go into the main house and take a look around. Off to one side of the house was a room that served as the live-in maid's quarters. Three steps took them down to a sunken living room. The atmosphere inside was warm and cozy. Adding to the richness of the interior was a gorgeous heated swimming pool with a grand view of the glistening city below.

CHAPTER THIRTEEN

SOMETHING WILD AND DANGEROUS

While Brian was back in London, Larry decided it was a good day to visit Dore Records[1] on Vine Street in Hollywood. Larry wanted to pitch a new song he had written, so he brought a demo tape of his recording. Lou Bedell, the owner of the label, was a friend of Larry's, so it was easy to set up an appointment. It was nice to see Lou, and he pitched his new song with confidence. Larry was in good spirits after the meeting, so he decided to walk across the street towards Wallich's Music City, his favorite music store to check out new record releases.

Larry stepped off the curb to cross the street just in time to see Diz Gillespie behind the wheel of a car that had stopped at the red light. "I'll be damned!" he mumbled. He quickly walked over to the passenger side of the vehicle and confronted Diz. Larry yelled at Diz about how horrible his behavior was the last time he saw him. "How dare you! You spiked my drink! I should punch you out!" Diz shrugged his shoulders and didn't appear to give a damn what Larry had to say. That confirmed what Larry suspected all the time; Diz took pleasure in doing what he did, just to hurt Larry.

Diz didn't hesitate to tell Larry he was on his way to New York and then to London to visit Brian at his home. Adding that he was invited, he taunted Larry by saying, "I guess you lost out on the kind of relationship Brian and I now have! Ha!" Larry wondered what Diz meant by that, as he and Brian remained very close. "In fact, he's my new meal ticket! Now don't get jealous, Larry!" When the light changed to green, he drove off, laughing in a sinister way. Larry was left standing in the middle of the crosswalk, stunned, red-faced, and pissed off.

After Diz sped off, Larry's first thought was of grave concern for Brian. Larry couldn't help but think about what Brian was getting himself into. He wondered if Brian was attracted to mean types. Perhaps that type was

---

1. Dore Records was a record label in Hollywood, located at 1481 Vine Street. The record company started 1958. Lew (Lou) Bedell owned and operated this record company along with his cousin Herb Newman. The company was named after his young son Dore. They released singles form the mid-1960's and were mostly pop and R&B records.

stimulating to him. Diz was just like a snake waiting quietly for the right moment to bite Brian in the balls. Larry felt a moment of hurt and a tinge of jealousy. It was hard to imagine that Brian didn't know he was getting into something wild and dangerous. Diz could certainly provide those temptations. Larry wondered if he should warn Brian before Diz arrived in England, but didn't want Brian to think he was jealous. The last thing he wanted to do was upset Brian or to appear insecure. He felt deeply for Brian and worked hard to keep a trusting and caring friendship as well.

CHAPTER FOURTEEN

BRIAN MEETS THE COLONEL

Since Brian had asked Larry during his last trip to help arrange a meeting with Colonel Tom Parker,[1] he made that his priority. The Beatles desperately wanted to meet Elvis and had been pestering Brian to make it happen. Larry hoped to impress Brian with some news about a successful contact and meeting plan, having set his goals on that direct path. After the evening at Laurence Harvey's house, Brian told Larry to make plans for the initial meeting to be in the Polo Lounge at the Beverly Hills Hotel. Larry was successful in obtaining a contact line directly to the Colonel and passed it along to Brian so he could call him directly, which he did.

Together again with Brian at a different Beverly Hills Hotel bungalow suite, presented a perfect opportunity for Larry to walk over to the Polo Lounge. The manager just happened to be standing in the doorway, and Larry motioned the need to speak with him in private. Larry told the manager that Mr. Brian Epstein and Col. Tom Parker would be meeting there for lunch and to make a reservation.

A couple of days later, they met for lunch as planned. The Colonel and Brian sized each other up before getting comfortable enough to start a serious conversation. The Colonel made numerous attempts at offering management advice to Brian. Before he would confirm a meeting between the Beatles and Elvis, the Colonel wanted Brian to come to his office at Paramount Studios. Brian agreed. The Polo Lounge meeting was a short one considering it was for lunch. Regardless, Brian left feeling he had accomplished his goal of arranging a "meet and greet" for the boys with the King of Rock and Roll, Elvis. The date and time were to be determined.

He returned to his bungalow and told Larry his thoughts about the Colonel being a peculiar man. Brian wasn't used to someone that acted like a loud, brash American. In reality, the Colonel wasn't even an American. Heck, he wasn't even a real Colonel! He told Larry that John (Lennon)

---

1. Colonel Tom Parker was born Andreas Cornelis von Kuijk in Holland. When he arrived in the United States he went by the name Thomas Andrew Parker. He was an "American carnie" that could never really get rid of the circus barker in his blood. He was born on June 26, 1909 and died in Las Vegas Nevada on January 27th 1997. He was considered to be a genius marketing man and responsible for Elvis Presley's successful career.

would get the biggest kick out of meeting Elvis and the Colonel. As John used to say, "There would be no Beatles without Elvis." Larry felt a sense of accomplishment in his assisting with the coordination of that initial meeting with the Colonel. He wished the credit was officially received, but that didn't happen. Brian respected the Colonel and said, "You can take the boy out of the circus, but you can't take the circus out of the boy!"

CHAPTER FIFTEEN

THE BEATLES COME TO TOWN

The Beatles planned to arrive on the West Coast in America on August 8, 1964 and Brian needed a place for them to stay while in Hollywood. Brian was very busy planning and making all the necessary travel arrangements. He managed to keep in touch with Larry by telephone, but his time was limited. Larry understood and only offered his help in whatever way needed.

At just about the same time but far away from the business of Rock n' Roll, two U.S. destroyers stationed in the Gulf of Tonkin off Vietnam radioed they had been fired upon by North Vietnamese forces. In response, President Lyndon B. Johnson requested permission from Congress to increase U.S. military presence in Indochina. A war was heating up and would impact our young men in the United States, pushing the teenage world into a social awakening of protests for peace rather than war.

Brian made reservations for the Beatles accommodations at the Ambassador Hotel in Los Angeles, but the hotel canceled their reservations stating an inability to handle the swarm of fans expected to turn out. They were afraid of liability and mass hysteria. It was incredibly difficult to find any luxury hotel for lodging due to the lack of guaranteed security, which was a massive obligation and task. Brian remembered that a British character actor named Reginald Owen[1] owned a mansion in Bel Air-Beverly Hills. Lionel Burt had introduced Reginald to Brian in England. Brian hoped an arrangement could be made since Reginald had made an offer that if the boys ever needed anything to contact him. So, in dire need, Brian contacted him and secured arrangements for Reginald's Bel Air mansion to be rented out to the Beatles.

The Beatles would be able to relax and prepare for their performance at the Hollywood Bowl.[2] It turned out to be a perfect arrangement all around. Once they arrived at the mansion, the Beatles were able to relax. They loved

1. Reginald Owen was an actor known for his British and American films and also television programs. He was born on August 5th 1887 in Wheat Hampstead, United Kingdom and died on November 5th 1072 in Boise, Idaho. He owned a house in Bel Air, California at 365 St. Pierre Road.
2. The Hollywood Bowl opened in 1922 on July 11th as one of the world's largest natural amphitheaters. The Hollywood Bowl had a long list of great performers and orchestras performing there along and including the Beatles. It's a Hollywood landmark to this very day.

the place, especially the outdoor pool, where they spent many fun-filled hours acting like wild children. Their Hollywood Bowl performance went down in music history and was recorded for future release many years later. It was the only official "live" album that the Beatles released.

CHAPTER SIXTEEN

A BOLD SEXUAL MOMENT

The sixties music revolution was running at full speed. Along with Beatle-mania, the mini-skirt would soon become the rave for many teenagers and young women. The world was on the precipice of change, but in August 1964, most people were still pretty square.

While the Beatles were safely tucked away, Brian contacted Larry for a get-together. They decided to test the waters at a popular club called the Melody Room,[1] which was on the Sunset Strip. That club was a mainstay in the Los Angeles music scene and was one of the oldest buildings on the Sunset Strip. As they enjoyed a few drinks, Brian moved in closer to Larry. They were reasonably well out of view in a small booth in the corner.

When no one was looking, Brian grabbed Larry's crotch under the table with gentle but firm cupping as if it belonged to him and him only. Brian enjoyed the bold gesture of a sexual moment in public with no one else knowing any better. His insatiable sex drive was kicking into full gear, and it wasn't long before they both shared the desire to head back to the bungalow to enjoy some wild and satisfying sex. That night they shared their bodies and their hearts. The bonds of love were forming as they surrendered to the need for sleep and dreams.

Waking up in bed together the next morning, they decided to celebrate that evening at a terrific Italian restaurant called The Villa Nova.[2] It was located on

---

1. Melody Room opened in 1951 on June 14th and was located at 8852 Sunset Blvd on the Sunset Strip in West Hollywood California. It was allegedly to have served as a gambling den for notorious gangsters like Mickey Cohen and Bugsy Siegel. The owners Pete and Billy Snyder were also rumored to be gangsters. It closed in 1969 and became Filthy McNasty's from 1973 until 1980, then became the Central during the 80's and finally The Viper Room in 1993. The Viper Room is the club where River Phones collapsed and later died at Cedars Sinai. The club was partly owned by Jonny Depp and Sal Jenco who also starred in the television series "21 Jump Street.
2. Villa Nova restaurant was located at 9015 Sunset Blvd on the Sunset Strip. It opened in 1935 and was owned by Allan Dale and his wife Charlotte. Allan was a silent star but didn't make the cross over to sound movies due to his accent. The Villa Nova in 1972 became the famous Rainbow Bar & Grill.

the Sunset Strip.[3] Larry called the restaurant in advance to make reservations. Besides having great menu choices, the Villa Nova's clientele was the cream of the crop in Hollywood. Feeling the sense of a glowing relationship made the evening very special indeed. Over dinner, Brian explained to Larry how much he wanted to introduce him to Derek Taylor. The thought of working for Brian, possibly on the books, thrilled Larry. He honestly looked forward to meeting Derek Taylor and hoped Brian wouldn't forget the offer.

3. Sunset Strip is only 1.6 miles long. It was a playground for the celebrities to visit nightclubs and bars with restaurants, hotels, nightclubs, and music venues and upscale retail shops.

CHAPTER SEVENTEEN

AN EVENING WITH FRANK SINATRA

One Saturday evening, Larry decided to take Brian to another Italian restaurant called Martoni's.[1] It was a favorite spot for people in the music business. At one point, Larry glanced over a few tables from where they were sitting and noticed two of KFWB's top radio personalities. Sitting there were Gene Weed and Bill Balance. Bill caught Larry's eye and walked over to their table to say hello. He recognized Brian Epstein at the table with Larry and waited for an introduction. Larry knew both of those DJ's, having met them at a social event recently at Dore Records. They were very popular DJ's and important to the music scene. Bill called out to Gene Weed, motioning him to walk over so he could say hello. Larry introduced them to Brian. After introduction pleasantries, Gene said to Brian, "Your Beatles are doing great and are now controlling all our airwaves, we love them! Keep up the good work!" Brian graciously thanked them both as they said good evening and returned to their table. Larry confirmed they were famous radio jocks in Los Angeles. Brian was elated with all the positive comments made, setting the tone for an even better evening.

Brian was even more fascinated when Larry told him how the Sinatra clan would hang out at Martoni's because of the real Italian atmosphere and great food. Hearing Sinatra's name triggered Brian's memory that Sinatra was performing in Las Vegas. He was a huge Sinatra fan and loved listening to Frank's albums. Larry could see the wheels turning in Brian's head and couldn't wait to hear what was coming next.

Sure enough, the next day, Brian couldn't stop thinking about Frank Sinatra. He wanted to fly over to Las Vegas and watch him perform live. Brian asked Larry to accompany him on the trip, stating they would need to leave rather quickly that afternoon. Since Sinatra was performing that evening, Larry promptly accepted

1. Martoni's was located in Hollywood at 1523 N. Cahuenga Blvd. It was owned by Sal Martoni and was nightly hang out for the music industry and disk jockey's during the 60's and 70's. It stayed open until Jan 17th 1994 and closed its doors because of the damage it received due to the Northridge earthquake.

the invitation. He was genuinely excited to take the trip with Brian. They had to pack an overnight bag quickly, and that meant Larry didn't have time to go home for more clothes. They drove to a men's shop down the street in Beverly Hills called Carroll and Co., and while Larry was willing to pay for a new suit, Brian wouldn't allow it. He bought Larry a stylish Italian suit.

They packed an overnight bag, and Larry called for a taxi to pick them up at the hotel. He left his Fiat parked on the street with hopes it would be safe until he returned. They arrived at LAX Airport just in time to catch the next flight to Las Vegas, Nevada.

The sun was setting in the hot, dry desert when the plane touched down in Las Vegas. That trip was a first time flying adventure for Brian and Larry. It was exciting to be in Vegas and stay at the Sands Hotel. They hailed a nearby taxi, and then they were off, heading towards the Sands Hotel. As the cab drove down the main strip, they saw the hotel in the distance with its iconic neon marquee in bold letters, 'Sands – A Place in the Sun.'

Checking into the hotel was an experience in itself. Brian was surprised when the management offered a complimentary suite for the night. Needing to freshen up, and also wanting to see the suite, they let the porters take their bags and show them where they would be staying tonight. Larry noticed how fashionable the porters were dressed and jokingly said the porters looked like the Beatles all dressed up in different suits. Brian's reaction came back faster than a speeding bullet. "No, absolutely not! How can you even joke about such a thing! My lads are dressed properly and with good taste, I've seen to that!" After a brief moment and noticing the stunned look on Larry's face, Brian figured out that he was kidding around. After that, Larry knew to tread lightly when he talked about the Beatles. There was no room for jokes about his lads. Arriving at their suite, Larry offered each porter one 45 record of "I Want to Hold Your Hand." While the younger porter was happy with a 45 of the world's most famous rock and roll group, the older porter motioned that he would rather have cash. Larry handed him a few dollars and told him to keep the 45 record as well.

They quickly freshened up, changed their clothes, and scurried off to the casino for some gambling fun. The ten-cent slot machines illuminated with green neon lights immediately got their attention, and they stopped to pull on those one-armed bandits. A waitress approached them and asked if they wanted a drink, so they ordered a gin and tonic rather than a usual wine. Slowly they made their way towards the showroom.

The Sands Hotel was strikingly more beautiful than ever as the scent of hot desert air was in the casino room. A pungent odor of women's perfume and an abundance of cigarette smoke hung mid-high above player's heads like an ever-present cloud. Splashes of red, green, and brown colors stood out in western style carpeting. Red leather chairs at gambling tables forced the interior to pop with excitement and invitation. The light beige laminate cashier counters were host to gold and brass pens that stood upright in black penholders for guests and gamblers to write checks for cash.

A tall, slender gentleman dressed in a dark blue fitted suit recognized Brian and approached him. With a deep but pleasing voice, he said the showroom entry fee was taken care of as well as their dinner and performance seats. Brian knew who was taking such good care of them.

Upon hearing that Brian Epstein would be in attending his show, Frank Sinatra made sure that Brian received first-class treatment. A maître d' walked them to a lovely booth positioned close to the stage. As the crowd began to seat themselves, Larry noticed how impeccably dressed they were. Tuxedos, gowns, furs, and lots of jewelry were proof that Sinatra was "chairman of the board." Larry and Brian looked spectacular as always.

Frank Sinatra gave the audience a fantastic performance, singing all his popular hit songs from a career unequaled for a male vocalist. The profoundly romantic lyrics moved Brian and Larry to the point that Brian reached under the table and gently held Larry's hand. It was the most romantic gesture and made Larry feel close and treasured. Larry recollected that Brian was reluctant to go backstage after the show and meet Mr. Sinatra. Brian didn't want Sinatra to feel obligated to pay him special attention. Instead, he sent his thanks and gratitude for a tremendous performance. Now, they had more time to play with Lady Luck.

The Sinatra show was over, but for Brian and Larry, the night was young, and the thrill of adventure beckoned them on. They headed back to the casino so Larry could play blackjack, and Brian could play baccarat, his favorite. Before he realized it, Larry ran out of the money he brought for gambling. He strutted over to the cashiers counter to cash a check for $800.00. To Larry's amazement, they accepted his check, and the cashier counted out $800.00 in crisp new bills. He suspected the company he kept contributed towards the ease at which he was able to cash a personal check. Being with Brian seemed to have its perks. Unfortunately, he didn't have $800.00 in his checking account, and if he didn't win some money, the check would bounce. Gambling fever took hold of Larry, and he thought he would win it all back. However, as the night developed, he continued to lose, and all his money stayed at the Sands.

Due to different game interests, Larry and Brian weren't spending time together. But a few hours later, Brian surprised Larry by tapping him on the shoulder as he stood behind him with a smile on his face. Although Larry had lost all the money, he managed to return a huge smile. Deciding to visit the lounge, they sat down at a small cocktail table. Brian popped a couple of white crisscross upper pills followed with a hard liquor drink. Larry joined in with gin and tonic. Larry reminisced that they stayed up the entire night, gambling away their winnings. He couldn't bring himself to tell Brian he'd lost over $800.00. Brian was very generous and spotted Larry some cash so he could continue gambling. The rest of the night was a frenzy of gambling. They were having so much fun they almost forgot about their morning flight back to Los Angeles.

The time came for them to quickly freshen up and arrange for the hotel limo to drive them to the airport. The flight back to Los Angeles was smooth and uneventful and allowed time for a catnap on the plane. But honestly, Larry said they were too wired to think of sleeping. A limousine waited for their arrival at LAX. They hurried into the back seat of the limo with the anticipation of having great sex after their all-night whirlwind. Once inside the bungalow, they dropped their bags, rushed into the bedroom, and crawled into the bed. They passed out before foreplay could even start, and they slept the entire day. Waking up as the sun began to set was a bit of a shock. Having lost track of time presented an opportunity to be cozy, snuggly, and warm in bed. Great sex worked itself into the evening hours, as they treasured moments of loving each other without a care in the world.

CHAPTER EIGHTEEN

A VISIT FROM THE MOB

Almost two weeks had passed since the trip to Las Vegas, and Brian once again traveled abroad to take care of business. Larry was relaxing and just hanging out in his Hollywood apartment when suddenly there was a loud knock at the front door. After a second and louder knock, Larry made his way over towards the door and answered. Two large-bodied no-neck Italians were standing outside. Larry was taken aback by the menacing look and refrigerator-sized men standing in front of him.

Aside from the guns that bulged in their waistband, they were nicely dressed in Italian Brioni suits. They told Larry that they had been looking for him, and they were relieved to find him at his home. Intimidated and stumbling for words, Larry asked them, "What kind of suits are you wearing?" One of the big guys said with a Brooklyn accent, "Touch the sleeve," and hesitantly Larry did. Suddenly one of the men snapped back and said abruptly, "Back to business Mr. Stanton," and then asked Larry, "When are you going to pay off your debt to the Sands Hotel in Las Vegas?" While waiting for an answer, one of the guys clenched his fist, giving off a fearful clicking sound. Larry felt a chill run up his spine.

Without a moment's hesitation, he replied, "I'll have the money within this week." The larger of the two men said, "Don't send it to us. Send a cashier's check directly to the Sands Hotel. We hope there isn't a need to see you again because if we do, it won't be pretty." Larry assured them one more time that he would have the money within the week. One of them responded, "Are you sure that's enough time for you?" Larry couldn't' answer fast enough. "You can bet on that!" Then the shorter and more massive of the two said, while staring at Larry with his shark eyes, "You're betting with your life, just remember, we know where to find you." Both men turned around and headed toward the black four-door Lincoln Continental double-parked in front of the apartment building. Larry shut the door behind them and almost fainted. In a loud voice, He said, "Oh, shit! How am I going to get that money?" He felt his heart beating fast, and rushed to the phone to call almost every co-worker and friend he knew to borrow the money. Miraculously, after combining what he acquired, along with his savings, he managed to get the entire $800.00, and luckily a day before the deadline.

CHAPTER NINETEEN

SAL MINEO'S NIGHTMARE

B
rian would call Larry by telephone no matter where in the world he was staying. They would speak to each other in lengthy conversations to catch up on their very different lives. The feeling of being able to talk and trust, regardless of distance, provided comfort whenever they communicated. After all, trust is earned and only comes with time. The telephone calls were their little secret, no one else knew.

Larry never had the opportunity to meet the Beatles but came close several times. He explained that Brian invited him to fly out and visit while he was in Nassau-Bahamas, shooting the movie *HELP* in February of 1965. "Help" was the 5th Beatle album, and it made for a good film while allowing the Beatles to travel to exotic locations. Brian thought it was a wonderful idea for Larry to be with him in the Bahamas. However, Larry's mother had a severe health problem, and regrettably, he couldn't take time off to meet up with Brian and finally meet the Beatles. It was a decision he regretted for the rest of his life.

With great personal satisfaction, Larry assisted Brian with scheduling his very private and secret social calendar. It was essential to avoid multiple calendar conflicts. That was a critical factor due to Brian's inner circle of administrative service employees that made arrangements for his artists and how that impacted him. Brian had to be sure his several calendars didn't conflict nor get revealed to the wrong people.

Sitting by the pool having drinks at the Beverly Hills Hotel one sun-drenched day, Brian told Larry how fond he was of another singing group called Herman's Hermits.[1] He also admired Little Richard.[2] Larry recalled that Brian explained how John Lennon was responsible for the introduction to Cilla Black[3] when she worked as a cloakroom attendant

---

1. Herman Hermits an English Rock band that was formed in Manchester, England in 1964. Peter Blair Denis Bernard Noone who was born on November 5th 1947 is the English singer-songwriter, guitarist and pianist and actor but he is best known as Herman of the very successful 1960's group.
2. Little Richard was born Richard Wayne Penniman on Dec 5th 1932 and is an American recording artist, singer-songwriter and actor. Little Richard was considered to be the architect of rock and roll and also an influence on the Beatles. He has been popular for over seven decades and was truly a charismatic showman. He recently passed away on 5/9/20 at 87 years old.
3. Cilla Black was another discovered artist by Brian Epstein while she was singing at the Blue Angel Jazz Club. Once he heard her he signed her to a contract and became his only female artist to

at the Liverpool club, "The Cavern." Larry quizzed Brian about his gifted eye for talent. "How do you recognize talent and sex appeal?" Brian responded, "Well, I have the emotional makeup of a fourteen-year-old girl, I suppose."

At the end of another glorious day with Brian, they went back to the bungalow. Brian gave Larry an original dub of "Ferry Cross the Mersey" by Gerry and the Pacemakers,[4] lovingly autographed by Brian. Larry treasured the disc but, sadly, was lost when moving from one place to another. Something he could kick himself in the rear for allowing it to happen. A few days later, Brian asked Larry to drop off some dubs or acetate recordings of new Beatles songs to Alan Livingston, the President of Capitol Records. Larry loved the Capitol Records tower building and loved to go there for any reason. He still says, "No one can be backed into a corner of that building since the building is round shaped."

By hanging out with Brian when he was in Los Angeles, Larry noticed he was running with a new circle of people, some of who were celebrities. Among them were Sal Mineo, and Lionel Bart.

The four guys hung out as often as possible. They shared an abundance of fun times and laughter and they also shared a secret about their sexual preferences.

There was another shared factor for Brian, Lionel, Sal, and Larry; they all felt the torture of mood swings and depression. That's one of the reasons their friendship flourished.

One evening when the stars aligned just right, they were all together at Brian's bungalow. With the lights off, the room glowed from candlelight and the crackling fire. They shared puffs from a neatly rolled reefer, popped pills, and sipped wine. As they sat on the couch by a small table, Sal shared a dream he had recently. In this dream, which was more of a nightmare, Sal, high on LSD, decided he would take a walk in Central Park. It was nighttime and very dark. Suddenly, a knife-wielding assailant that was hiding in the darkness confronted him. The assailant lunged towards Sal thrusting the knife at his face. Sal tried to defend himself, and ultimately was able to grab the knife from the man. Sal killed the attacker with a

---

represent in 1963.

4. Gerry and the Pacemakers was an English group in 1960's. The group was also managed by Brian Epstein came from Liverpool, England. George Martin at Abbey Road Studios produced the band's records for Columbia Records. Gerry Marsden formed the group in 1959 with his brother Fred. They were competitive to the Beatles and played in the same circles in Hamburg Germany and Liverpool. They were the second band to sign with Brian Epstein. This was the first group that Brian had a number one record with on the UK Charts. "How Do You Do It," "Like it" and "You'll Never Walk Alone." They were the second most successful pop group form Liverpool.

single blow, stabbing him in the chest. When Sal woke up, he thought it really happened; it seemed so real.

It's ironic that a few years later, in West Hollywood, Sal Mineo met a tragic end. He was stabbed to death in a dark alley while he was high on LSD. Coincidence, premonition, or destiny, Larry still thinks of that dream as one that became a reverse reality. What a horrible way to die!

Sal and Lionel accompanied Brian and Larry out to dinner several times. On one of those occasions at a French restaurant called The Bistro[5] in Beverly Hills, everyone at the table realized how naïve Larry was about French cuisine. While reviewing menu choices, Larry asked Brian and their waiter to explain vichyssoise. Brian replied, "It's just cold potato soup." Larry laughed it off and commented that while he didn't know about vichyssoise or French food, he thanked God for American hamburgers and ketchup. With every experience, Brian and Larry shared, laughter, good food, fun, and love came right along with it.

Even though Brian's schedule was dominated by music-related business, he and Larry managed to spend incredible quality time together. It was common knowledge amongst their few friends that whenever Brian was in Los Angeles, he stayed at the Beverly Hills Hotel, and usually in one of the bungalows. Brian would contact Larry before he left London to let him know his arrival plans so that Larry could free up his time and set up some social arrangements. If Larry and Brian wanted to have a few drinks without dining, they would often go to the Frolic Room[6] on Hollywood Boulevard, a block down from Capitol Records. There were a few other bars on Santa Monica Blvd. they would haunt as well. But eating good food and enjoying each other's company was always a top priority, next to sex, of course.

Brian recommended they have dinner at La Scala restaurant. That evening would prove to be another memorable one. It was just the two of them out to enjoy a good meal. The restaurant was crowded, but they were

5. The Bistro was located at 246 North Cannon Drive in Beverly Hills. The owner was Kurt Nikals, who also owned the Bistro Garden. He catered to celebrities of the Film and Television industry as well as high society. Today it is Mastro's restaurant.
6. The Frolic Room is located next to the Pantages Theater at 6245 on Hollywood Blvd. Hollywood, CA 90028. It opened to the public in 1934 as Bob's Frolic Room. It's been the location for many television shows and Films.

still seated right away. While reviewing the menu and waiting for a bottle of wine to arrive, they happened to look up just in time to see an actor named Raphael Campos walk in with two very feminine looking males. Raphael Campos was a breakout star that acted in the movie *Blackboard Jungle*. He was also married to Diana Washington, who was eleven years older than Raphael. She was considered a big star, had been married seven times prior, was a pianist, and Queen of the Blues.

CHAPTER TWENTY

Diz, The Rough Tiger

When Brian was back in England and extremely busy with the typical business of the day, he always made travel arrangements for his various acts via his administrative support. Brian would show up to meet and support his acts, assuring all was in order as planned and off to a good start. After business finished, he would take off to do his own thing. One item of note is that Brian kept his personal affairs and travel arrangements very private. It's as if Brian led two lives. That was one topic of conversation each time Larry and Brian talked, either in person or by telephone.

Since that last party, Brian hosted in the bungalow at the Beverly Hills Hotel, and when Larry ran into Diz at the Vine Street intersection in Hollywood, there had been no mention of Diz's name between Brian and Larry. Out of no-where, an unexpected visitor surprised Brian. It was John 'Diz' Gillespie. Brian had to think for a moment before he vaguely remembered making an offer for Diz to come to London anytime. He then remembered writing down his flat address and telephone number. Diz had decided to accept the offer and now wanted to immerse himself into Brian's world. Of course, Brian was immediately interested in nurturing the affair since it was standing right in front of him.

From the moment Diz arrived in London, Brian was utterly captivated and smitten. Diz was an extremely handsome young man and seemed to titillate Brian in the most provocative and tempting ways. After a short time, Brian took him in and provided for Diz, setting him up financially, buying him a new wardrobe, and signing him on at NEMS as his latest discovery. Brian had become Diz's "sugar-daddy" providing him with all the comforts, needs, and desires he wanted. But Brian didn't think of it that way. He thought Diz might be the one he'd been yearning for his entire life. Brian was a fixer, and while he knew Diz was flawed, he felt he could change him for the better.

With Diz spending time with him in England, Brian had to make sure that he wouldn't be around when he was conducting business. Their relationship started with flirtatious enticements, wild sex, and romantic companionship, but it wasn't long before problems set in. The relationship Brian had with John "Diz" Gillespie had become a 'rough tiger' kind of sexual bond. It had grown into a tumultuous relationship filled with physical and mental abuse. Diz, according to Larry, was finally in a position to use Brian anyway he could. Diz was doing precisely what he told Larry he would.

Things had gotten out of hand with Diz. According to NEMS Director and confidant of Brian's Peter Brown, Diz came close to killing Brian one night. Brian signed Diz to the NEMS stable of artists and showered him with a new wardrobe and glorious press releases. He also paid Diz a weekly salary even though Diz did nothing to earn his keep. They spent many evenings together at Brian's flat ingesting large amounts of uppers, Tuinals, and cognac. Mostly these drugged out nights ended in violence, complete with breaking vases and mirrors. One night, Diz worked himself into a rage over money and drugs. When Brian ordered him out of the house, Diz ran into the kitchen, grabbed the largest knife he found and held it to Brian's throat. While the knife pressed hard against Brian's jugular vein, Diz emptied Brian's wallet of all the cash he had and left. Brian swore he would never see Diz again.

Brian shared his misplaced happiness as well as the painful episodes with Larry, calling him long distance at all hours of day or night. On one international call, Brian told Larry that Diz always caused him pain, hurting him both emotionally and physically. He confessed that Diz stole from him when he was away from home for a meeting or traveling for business. Unfortunately, that had occurred numerous times already. Larry found it hard to believe Brian would leave himself so open and vulnerable. Larry felt sad upon hearing that Brian was suffering. He now had confirmation that Diz was an evil guy. Larry had been feeling that for a long time. What he couldn't figure out was why Brian couldn't see through the thin veil of fake sincerity. One could only suspect the weight of desire and love was overwhelmingly to blame.

On one occasion, when Brian had to leave London on business, Diz had a wild street party at his house. Diz and his gang of hoodlums drank all of Brian's fine wine and champagne collection and trashed the inside of his house. "It's difficult to know all that was stolen or broken because those undesirable people went into every area within my flat," said Brian. That incident caused a big tiff between Diz and Brian's household servant Lonnie Trimble. Lonnie knew what was happening, as he had to clean up the mess. Diz didn't lift a finger! Needless to say, Lonnie was not a fan of dear Diz. Neither was Larry, but he respectfully stayed quiet and just listened to what Brian had to say.

Brian explained that Lonnie would question him about Diz, such as, "why do you put up with such behavior, Brian?' Those queries and comments only upset him even more. Brian would often take it out on Lonnie rather than appreciate his honesty and caring inquires. Eventually, when Lonnie opened up to Larry about that problem, it was a classic case of shoot the messenger. Brian refused to open his eyes and ears to the real person that Diz was. Larry had an image pass through his mind of the three wise monkeys; 'Mizaru - see no evil, Kikazaru - hear no evil, and Iwazaru - speak no evil.'

CHAPTER TWENTY-ONE

A DANGEROUS SOCIOPATH

One early Hollywood morning, Larry decided to call Brian in England, just to see how he was doing. When the overseas operator placed the call, Lonnie answered and accepted the reverse charges. That was the procedure Brian recommended so they could communicate often and privately.

Although they had never spoken, Lonnie was aware of Larry from friendly conversations with Brian. Now that he was finally speaking to Larry, they talked openly about issues that concerned them both. Larry sensed that Lonnie wanted to get some matters off his chest. The first comment Lonnie made was that Brian wouldn't let anyone get close to him and into his private space. He was starting to close himself off from friends he had known for years.

Lonnie understood that Brian and Larry had a special kind of relationship. Outside of Brian's infatuation with Diz, Larry was closest to the type of relationship Brian dreamed of having. Teasingly Lonnie blamed Larry for introducing Diz to Brian. He quickly added that Brian was a grown man and responsible for his choices. Who he chose to get involved with was up to Brian. Larry wasn't to blame; Diz was a guest of his roommate Jerry. Regardless, that comment stung Larry, and he never forgot it.

According to Lonnie, no one other than Brian cared for Diz, and Larry couldn't agree with him more. It was apparent Diz used Brian, taking advantage of his tender heart, his kindness, and his yearning for love. Lonnie was more than just a servant. He was also a person Brian confided with about the closeted gay world. Both felt such sadness having no choice but to hide their love away from the outside world. The oppressive and frightening laws in England resulted in enormous suffering that strangled the basic need of a loving relationship that was every human beings right. Larry made sure Lonnie was aware that the oppression of Gays was no different in the United States.

Once Brian asked Lonnie how he and his partner Patrick was such a happy couple. He responded that it's easy when two friends respect and love each other. They focused on the care and nurturing necessary to maintain a healthy relationship. Larry and Lonnie agreed that Brian was his own worst enemy and a magnet for people that used him in destructive ways. Brian possessed a dark side, an insatiable lust for humiliation and rough sex. No matter how debased Brian got, he could not fill the emptiness and loneliness that haunted him. He would often bring his rough boys to the house. Once, Lonnie asked Brian if he felt nervous bringing those types into his private world. Brian replied, "Oh, no! They wouldn't hurt me. I'm Brian Epstein, and there would be consequences." That comment seemed out of character for Brian. He would listen to Lonnie's advice from time to time, but when it came to lover boy Diz, Brian was deaf.

Lonnie continued their conversation by telling Larry about one particular morning while he was at Brian's home working. That's when he first encountered Diz, and he vividly remembered how Brian seemed to be glowing. He and Diz pranced around playing house all weekend. Lonnie thought "best wishes" that this new person in Brian's life might become a steady companion and lover, making Brian happy. It turned out that concerns set in rather quickly. "When he was being a 'good Diz,' everything was great. But then he suddenly turned into a 'bad Diz' as if schizophrenic, and things got ugly, really fast."

Both of them would fight about anything. Many fights involved drugs that Diz wanted to consume. Diz was continually high, stoned, or speeding on amphetamines, and he wanted Brian to do the same. It was of no consequence if Diz was throwing his life down the tubes, he was a loser and hustler, a party boy. Brian, on the other hand, had immense responsibilities. He had a very public business and couldn't afford to be seen messed up on drugs. If they weren't fighting about drugs, they fought about the boys and women Diz brought into Brian's flat. Brian wanted his home to be a special place for the two of them, not for every Tom, Dick, and Harry Diz brought around. As if that wasn't enough, Diz told Brian he was bisexual and was tired of playing his gay stud. He wanted to venture out with a variety of sex partners. Those words stung and tortured Brian like a hundred bees swarming around him.

Lonnie shared another story about a wild party incident that pushed him past holding back his temper. Lonnie showed up to work one morning when Brian was out of town only to find boys and girls sprawled out all over the apartment. When Lonnie found Diz amongst the pile of bodies, he pulled him off and said to him, "You're making my life a misery! You're creating way too much work for me with your party friends! And by the way, you are not playing your role the right way. It's your business, and you don't have to be in love with Brian, but at least show him some affection and respect. That would make him happy. Don't you care about that? You're making his life miserable too!"

Larry was saddened upon hearing about that incident. He wanted to know if Lonnie ever told Brian about that party and face-to-face talk with Diz. Sadly, that didn't happen. Furthermore, Diz didn't want any advice from him and would ignore Lonnie as best he could to avoid confrontation. Brian started to treat Lonnie differently, becoming disrespectful and argumentative. Brian was taking all his frustrations out on Lonnie. Larry felt deeply touched because he suspected it might be the last phone conversation he would have with Lonnie. Brian wasn't treating him right and had become a different kind of boss. It was time to leave. It was just a matter of time.

With Larry's undivided attention, Lonnie spoke about another horrible event that was, unfortunately, witnessed by Brian's parents. "One evening, Lonnie continued, Brian wanted me to cook a lovely dinner for his mother and father so they could meet Diz. The menu included a large Dover Sole fish, green veggies, potatoes and parsley, and simple vanilla pudding. Halfway through dinner Diz and Brian started to bicker back and forth. Diz deliberately knocked over his glass of wine, stood up with nostrils flared, and in front of Brian's parents said something really nasty to Brian. Then he stormed out of the flat. Queenie and Harry, Brian's parents, were speechless, not knowing what to say or do. After sitting still for quite a few moments, they decided the evening was finished. They apologized to Brian for having to leave in such a way but thought it best. Brian was so embarrassed and humiliated, even though his mother and father tried to console him, telling him it wasn't his fault."

Just then, Brian walked in the front door, and Lonnie abruptly asked Larry to hold on the line for a moment. He announced that the American named Larry was on the phone. While on hold and waiting for Brian to pick up the phone, thoughts flew around in Larry's head about how out of control the relationship with Diz was getting. It was painful for Larry to hear what Lonnie exposed, but he just had to accept it, for now. After a few moments on hold, Brian picked up the receiver and in a very joyful voice said hello. Larry felt the sincerity of Brian's happiness to hear from him. But it wasn't long before the tone of Brian's voice changed to a beaten-down softness as he started to inform Larry about how awful Diz was acting and the things he had done to hurt him emotionally. Diz had become a very mean and hurtful person, using horrible words, and displaying violent behavior.

He told Larry he knew the relationship was poisonous, and it was breaking his heart. Still, it was too difficult for him to break loose from Diz. There was an attraction towards Diz that he just couldn't control. He admitted a loss of willpower in dealing with his feelings for Diz. He was afraid, vulnerable, and sensed he was losing it emotionally. Then Brian shared the story about his parents coming to dinner, adding that Diz acted in such an inexcusable manner. Larry reacted as if he knew nothing about it, saying how sorry he was it happened. It was tearing up his insides not to lash out at Brian.

Brian listened to Larry's advice for ending the hold Diz had on him, but those words of wisdom just went in one ear and out the other. All Diz would have to do was crawl shamelessly back, and Brian would melt in his arms. Like molten lava, Diz was smothering Brian with his poisonous version of love, and Brian became increasingly intoxicated by the emotions that took over and controlled him. He was obsessed with Diz and anything he said or wanted became more important to Brian than the truth. Theirs was not what a loving relationship should be.

Brian was consuming pills, and that didn't help his emotional imbalance, it only added fuel to the fire. The deeper he traveled down that rabbit hole, the deeper into emotional hell he went. Larry said that he would be happy to drop everything and fly out to London if Brian wanted him to. The question was did Brian even want Larry to be there? Only time would tell.

CHAPTER TWENTY-TWO

A TICKET TO RIDE

Despite the stress, drugs, and heartache, Brian was still able to manage the world's greatest rock band, as well as the many other artists he had signed. Nevertheless, he became more emotionally erratic each day. From the moment Brian introduced Larry to Derek Taylor,[1] there was a shared concern for Brian. Larry found Derek to be personable, and they got along well. He was also concerned about Brian's emotional state of mind due to mounting problems related to everyday business, but didn't think it was all that serious. That's because he didn't know all the details and issues. Larry said that while Derek acted very professional and seemed generally sincere, he joked about Brian's depressions and instability in a way that bothered Larry. People closest to Brian would make fun of him behind his back, and whenever Brian overheard those comments, it filled him with doubts and self-loathing. His confidence was crumbling.

At one point, Derek and Brian explored investing in shopping malls in various cities in the United States. Larry was given the opportunity to participate in those investments, but he didn't have the extra money to invest. He believed Brian was responsible for planting that seed in Derek's mind. Brian was always trying to reward him for his friendship in some way or another. But Larry wasn't looking for those types of reward or monetary gains. He was more concerned about Brian's wellbeing.

Larry remembered another enjoyable outing and dinner at Musso & Frank[2] restaurant, one of Hollywood's

1. Derek Taylor was an English Journalist, writer, publicist and record producer, known for being the press officer to the Beatles. He was a gifted publicist creating several promotional campaigns such as "The Beatles Are Coming" He also helped stage the Monterey Pop Festival which proceeded Woodstock and was is considered the first major outdoor mega concert. He also was the ghostwriter for " Cellarful of Noise" a book that is the title of Brian Epstein's autobiography.

2. Musso & Franks is Hollywood's oldest restaurant located at 6667 Hollywood Boulevard, Los Angeles CA 90028. Entrepreneur Frank Toulet joined forces with Oregon restaurateur Joseph Musso. They hired French Chef Jean Rue who created the menu, and the restaurant opened in 1919. After 100 years it is still open and is known for their unparalleled service and Hollywood's

oldest restaurants located right in the middle of Hollywood Boulevard. They pulled into the parking lot behind the restaurant, and instead of using the valet service he parked his Fiat car himself. Going into Musso & Frank by way of the back door and then down the steep stairs they walked past a seating area up to the front where the Maître d' was standing at his dais. Other than the Maître d' nobody paid them any attention; no wild Beatle fans or press. Larry convinced the Maître d' to seat them in the same booth the famous silent star Charlie Chaplin would always request while dining. That booth is upfront and close to the main entrance and tucked discreetly into a corner.

Brian fell in love with that restaurant and told Larry it reminded him of some of the restaurants in London that had an old-world charm. When the first bottle of wine was opened, Brian excitedly offered a toast to Larry. "Well, here's to you for picking sides on a record! Remember when you said that 'Ticket to Ride'[3] was a hit for the 'A' side and in your opinion would be a number one hit? Well, for your information, 'Ticket to Ride' is top of the charts. You know your music! Good ears, my man, Good ears! You are right as rain!" To be acknowledged by Brian in that way, wow! It sure made for some great feelings, and Larry felt like he was on cloud nine. Receiving confirmation and gratitude from Brian meant the world to him and felt higher than if he smoked the best refer; he glowed for days!

---

finest cuisine.
3. Ticket To Ride," was the A Side and "Yes It Is" was the B-side of a single that was released becoming the Beatles seventh consecutive number one hit in the UK and the 3rd consecutive number one his in the US. "Ticket To Ride" was also featured in the movie *HELP.*

CHAPTER TWENTY-THREE

You Can't Win Them All

Brian's schedule became more frenzied as the artists he managed needed his attention. His main concern was The Beatles, and they were riding a tsunami of top #1 hits in the U.S. and Britain. Whenever Brian was in Los Angeles, he did his best to combine business with pleasure, and that meant contacting Larry. Larry was always excited when Brian came to town. He surprised Larry with a phone call one day and said, "Guess what? I'm back, and I'd love to see you if you have the time. Why don't you pick me up in your car and let's go to dinner? We can go anywhere you would like. And by the way, I'm in a bungalow at the same place." Larry responded right away that he would arrive in forty-five minutes. Brian's response was "Smashing!" In a flash, Larry pulled himself together and walked directly to his Fiat parked right out in front. He hopped into the car and released the brake so the car would roll forward, not taking a chance it wouldn't start. When he popped the clutch, the engine sputtered to life. It was a fairly short distance to Brian's bungalow. As he arrived, Larry was surprised to see Brian. By coincidence, he had walked outside just as Larry arrived.

Brian jokingly said, "I miss having to push your funny car to get it started. I never do things like that unless I'm with you." Larry was pleased to see Brian smile and said, "I'm sure you'll have plenty of chances to push my funny car, no doubt about that." They both burst out in laughter. While sitting in the car, they decided to stay at the hotel rather than drive anywhere.

Brian suggested they walk over to the Polo Lounge[1] and have dinner. Now there would be more time after dinner for fun and relaxation.

Upon entering the Polo Lounge, Brian immediately took notice of two very handsome young men sitting in a booth chatting. Larry saw them too and knew what Brian had in mind. Brian asked Larry to invite them to

1. Polo Lounge wasn't a private club but it was exclusive. It was where celebrities would go not to get noticed. The Polo Lounge was a premier dining spot in Beverly Hills. It was decorated in peachy pink with dark green booths that featured a plug in phone. Hernando Courtright ran the Polo Lounge between the 30's and 40's had a friend named Charles Wrightsman, who led a national champion polo team. Wrightsman felt uncomfortable keeping the team trophy, a silver engraved bowl, in his own home where few people would have the chance to see it. Mr. Courtright, after hearing his friend's dilemma and recognizing how to turn a lemon into lemonade, offered to display the bowl in the hotel's bar. Hence the name "The Polo Lounge."

their table. Better yet, to the bungalow for a drink after dinner. As Larry walked over to their table, two beautiful women walked into the lounge and joined the handsome young men. Stopping dead in his tracks, Larry made an about-face and returned to Brian, saying, "You can't win them all, Brian!

"You almost gave us away, Lauren," declared Brian. "Those two are going to have a good time tonight."

While sitting in those famous large comfortable booths, tables adorned with brilliant white tablecloths; Larry observed that Brian didn't look as fresh as he usually did. His first thought was the lighting in the room. But as he focused in on the pallor of Brian's face, a sting of concern set in. He hadn't noticed that appearance outside in the daylight, but now inside, he looked worn down with his skin color looking sallow and somewhat jaundiced in tone. Just before they ordered from the menu, Brian swallowed a small white pill, drinking it down with a glass of water. Brian began sharing details about a sad event, and it involved none other than Diz Gillespie. Diz had stolen something priceless from Brian, and to make matters worse, he was treating him in horrible, demeaning ways.

The relationship between Brian and Diz was getting worse. Larry felt his stomach tighten, afraid to hear what it was about, and not sure of how he would react this time. Slowly Brian looked at Larry and said, "I'm heartbroken Larry, and I'm physically and emotionally exhausted."

Diz did the unthinkable; he stole contracts and acetates of Beatle songs. The acetates were not the master tapes; they were kept in another location in England. It would be extremely embarrassing for Brian if it came out that Beatle items were stolen from his home. It could damage his relationship with the Beatles. Larry decided to ask a ridiculous question. "Do you know who stole those items, Brian?" What stunned Larry was Brian's response. "I believe we both know who the thief was!"

CHAPTER TWENTY-FOUR

LAST KISS

One night after having smoked a joint, Larry decided to visit a well-known 24-hour market known as the Hollywood Ranch Market. It wasn't far, right on the corner of Fountain Avenue and Vine Street. Across the way was 'Villa Elaine', a well-known hotel that housed many struggling performers and actors of the day.

As he walked around the market, Larry bumped into a few guys he knew that worked in production on the new *Regis Philbin Television Show*.[1] One guy remembered that Larry and Brian Epstein were friends and mentioned that the show would enjoy having Brian be a guest. He replied that he would check Brian's schedule and then see if Brian was interested. He assured a response as soon as he could touch base with Brian.

Larry was having a bite to eat when another friend walked over and joined him.

Dobie Gray[2] was an aspiring young and handsome black singer from Texas. He moved to Hollywood to become a recording star. Dobie wore a long trench coat with hidden pockets that served multiple purposes. When times were tough, Dobie and Larry would meet at the market to steal food to eat. While Larry was on the lookout, Dobie would fill his pockets; at times, they switched places. After a short walk to Larry's, they divided the goods. Survival was the name of the game, and you did what you had to do. Larry wasn't proud of having to steal, and he certainly

---

1. Regis Philbin was born Regis Frances Xavier Philbin in the Bronx, New York City on August 25th 1931. He was an American media personality, actor and singer known for hosting talk and game shows since the 1960s. His first exposure to television was on his Regis Philbin Show, and then got national exposure in 1967 as Joey Bishop's sidekick on the Joey Bishop Show.

The Regis Philbin Show lasted from 1964 to 1965, and was produced and filmed on Vine Street at the Hollywood Playhouse on La Mirada and Vine Street. This show replaced the Steve Allen Playhouse Theatre, which was located at 1228 North Vine Street in Hollywood. The theatre was originally named the La Mirada Theatre in 1926, and later the Film Arte Theatre in 1928, and then it became the Linkletter Playhouse in 1957. This Hollywood location was also famous for the "Steve Allen Show," which was the original Tonight Show. It's where the bits for all late night shows were created and then would be copied for generations to come. The show "You Bet Your Life" starring Groucho Marx was also filmed there

2. Dobie Gray an American singer songwriter, whose musical career covered soul, country, pop and musical theater. In 1965 he had a hit record with "The In Crowd" and "Drift Away" which was a big hit in 1973. He was born by then name of Lawrence Darrow Brown on July 26th 1940 and died on December 6th 2011

hoped Brian would never find out. Eventually, Dobie achieved great career and financial success. Those were some tough financial times for Larry as well as Dobie. Somehow they managed to survive it all. Later that week, Larry reached Brian by phone and extended the invitation to appear on the new Regis Philbin Show. With very little thought put into it, Brian gladly agreed to do the show. He thought the exposure would be good, not only for him but for all his clients as well. With Brian's approval under his belt, Larry called his friend at the production office and confirmed he would deliver Brian Epstein to the show. When the day arrived for Brian to appear on the show, Larry had a wonderful time in assisting Brian throughout the entire production. Brian was impressed with how he took charge and mentioned he would be happy for a repeat appearance if that request surfaced in the future. The show, featuring Eartha Kitt[3] aired on November 9, 1964

After the taping, Larry dismissed the limousine to take Brian back to his bungalow, and instead, they walked across the street to the 24-hour Hollywood Ranch Market. Brian bought a couple of ripe looking grapefruits for breakfast. Larry suggested they walk a few blocks to his apartment before driving to the hotel. Surprisingly none of the roommates were home when they arrived, making for a more comfortable evening. It was Brian's last night in Los Angeles, so he suggested dinner at the Bistro in Beverly Hills.

The Bistro Restaurant was located on North Canon Drive, not far from the hotel. Owned by Kurt Niklas, it was an elegant nightspot, and on any given night, any one of importance could be found hobnobbing with their fellow wizards. It must have been visually funny to see them pulling up in front of The Bistro in that little Fiat. Larry tossed his keys to the valet as if he was driving a Roll-Royce.

Famished, they ordered right away, choosing the grilled salmon dinner with baked potato and crisp green salad. While taking time to savor their meal, a man by the name of Alan Livingston – Vice President of Capitol Records approached their table. Just wanting to say hello and convey congratulations to Brian with regards to the Beatles success, Alan then asked if Brian would be in town for a while. Brian avoided an answer to his question by way of an introduction to Larry. With no response, Alan said he hoped to see Brian again during his visits within the U.S. and extended

---

3. Eartha Kitt was an American Singer, Actress, Dancer, Activist and Author and songwriter. She had two top ten record hits in 1953. She was born in cotton fields in South Carolina on January 17 1927 and died December 25, 2008 in Weston, Connecticut. Orson Wells called her "The most exciting girl in the world."

an invite up to his office in the Capitol Records building. Alan left shortly after extending good wishes and a good evening.

Out of nowhere, Hank Sanicola walked up and said hello to Larry, apologizing for the interruption. A quiet evening together was not to be. Larry immediately introduced Hank to Brian. Speaking very politely, Hank said he was still interested in Larry's singing career and recommended he give the office a call for an appointment. Larry thought about how it must appear to Hank in seeing him with Brian Epstein. It took Brian by surprise, too, as he heard of Mr. Sanicola and of the talent he represented. But, Brian had no idea about Larry's hidden singing career. Surprise!! After Hank left them to finish eating, Larry observed how taken back Brian was. He had a bewildered look on his face. Larry explained his love for singing and revealed the many attempts made to succeed in the business. He said to Brian that the last thing he wanted to do was bring up his singing career desires and giving any impression that it had anything to do with their continued relationship. Larry spoke to Brian with such sincerity and honesty that Brian understood, and he responded, "Well, maybe I ought to hear you sing sometime." Once again, Larry reiterated that he had no intention of mentioning it, as it had nothing to do with the kind of relationship they had. Larry reached under the table and grabbed Brian's hand with a tight squeeze. He hoped Brian trusted his explanation and sincerity. Larry smiled and said, "But, if you ever want me to sing you a lullaby, just ask."

Larry wanted Brian to get a good night's sleep before leaving the next day for an early flight out from LAX Airport. While taking out cash to pay the restaurant bill, Brian leaned in towards Larry's ear, speaking softly with a promise to stay in touch as often as he possibly could. Brian whispered that Larry would never know how really special he was.

Back at the bungalow, Brian gave Larry a huge good-bye hug along with a kiss full of deep affection and feelings. Larry fought his desire to sit down and get comfortable, really wanting Brian to get all the rest he could get. Sex was out of the question! Before Larry left the bungalow, Brian gave him an autographed copy of his book *Cellar Full Of Noise*. Brian thought Larry would enjoy the read, telling him that Derek Taylor did a damn good job of impersonating him…in the literal sense. Brian had prepared in advance a sweet personalized note. While handing over the book to Larry, he told him John made many jokes about the book's title, saying it should have been called "Queer Jew" or a "Cellar Full of Boys." He laughed, but in reality, those words stung and hurt him. John didn't bother to think about how much it hurt Brian.

Thankful for the book, Larry had a brief moment of feeling abandonment pains with Brian leaving so early the next day. He wanted to stay the night and relish in the beauty of what they mutually shared. Larry returned a warm and long farewell kiss, a firm hug, and slowly opened the door to leave. He waved good-bye and blew a kiss as Brian closed the door. Larry walked to his car, choked up with feelings, and wondered about the likelihood of not seeing Brian ever again. Feeling out of his league, he realized Brian was part of a different world, no matter how hard he tried to imagine the possibilities! Those feelings of loss, a relationship he might not find again, tore the insides of his heart and stomach. Brian didn't say good-bye forever, yet Larry felt as if the love of his life had slipped out of his fingers.

Those moments spent with Brian were the most exciting times he ever had. Until they could be together again, all he could do was dream about it. The drive home was long and slow, with the wind blowing through his hair. With an overwhelming emptiness that only time would heal, the drive back was very lonely indeed. At that moment, Larry had no idea it would be the last time he and Brian would ever see each other.

CHAPTER TWENTY-FIVE

THE MURDEROUS KRAY TWINS

With Brian back in England, he kept in contact with Larry by telephone. On the downside, the calls were expensive, but on the upside, they were therapeutic for both of them. Brian and Larry felt better afterward, and when moments of depression crept in, there was someone to talk to and listen. Larry was elated that Brian didn't forget about him; it was a long distant relationship.

Even though Brian was not in Los Angeles, he continued to have Larry run some small business errands and contact people that were local and, therefore, easier for Larry. Those were tasks he ordinarily would ask his secretary in England to take care of, but Brian wanted to keep Larry busy and perhaps, on a slight emotional leash.

Since Brian kept his private activities from those around him, he trusted Larry with handling some of his confidential affairs. Larry didn't want Brian to feel as if he was obligated to him in any way other than friendship. He cared about him deeply, and that's why he helped Brian with whatever he needed.

During one of their overseas calls, Brian told Larry there was a new lover in his life named Michael. Larry remembered hearing the name before during a prior conversation with Lonnie. While not going into details about their relationship, Brian did inform Larry that Michael was kind and sensitive. Larry was pleased to hear some happy relationship news from Brian. Quickly changing the subject, Larry asked if Brian was still in contact with Diz. Brian only commented that they occasionally kept in touch. The conclusion Larry came up with was that Brian and Diz still had a tortuous on and off-again relationship. Larry's gut feeling told him Brian was hiding something, but he let it go, not wanting to be upsetting.

Larry was curious about Brian's private social life and what he did for fun. Brian remembered a club he went to in the past named Esmeralda's Barn,[1] a club owned by the infamous Kray "twin" brothers[2] in London.

1. Esmeralda's Barn was a nightclub in Wilton Place, Knightsbridge, London, and was owned by the Kray twins from 1960 until its closure in 1963. The Kray's used the club as a way of expanding their criminal activities into London's West End. The club allegedly became a useful front for the Krays criminal activities, including the prostitution of young men whom they use to entrap blackmail targets.
2. Kray Brothers: There were three Kray brothers, Charles James Kray (July 9, 1927, April 4, 2000),

The Kray twins were notorious gangsters that ruled London's East End by fear, intimidation, torture, and murder. Ronnie and Reggie Kray were feared, and they were able to mingle with an elite group from politics and entertainment. Brian informed Larry that he initially met Ronnie Kray at a club in London, and the next thing he knew the Kray brothers were attempting to get very close to him, especially after the brothers found out about his affair with John "Diz" Gillespie. The fact they had any interest in his very private affairs seemed strange and was very disturbing to Brian. The Krays would question him about his nightlife and business affairs, as well as inquiring about the Beatles and other acts he managed. They wanted to know as much about Brian as they could. In fact the Krays had gone so far as to notify Glasgow crime lord Arthur Thompson[3] that they were blackmailing Brian Epstein and were going to take the Beatles from him. Thompson apparently convinced the twins that the Beatles career would go downhill fast if they became associated with the Krays. They settled for blackmailing him for cash.

Fear crept into Brian's thoughts. The Kray brothers wanted to muscle in on his business. He told Larry it was a mystery to him how much they knew about his relationship with Diz, but suspected it had something to do with another popular location called the Clermont Club.[4] Perhaps some of the high society clientele that frequented that club shared in spreading gossip. The Clermont Club was a gambling casino with very influential customers that included aristocrats such as Lord Boothby.[5] Brian observed that Boothby

Ronald "Ronnie" Kray (October 24, 1933 –March 17, 1995), and Reginald "Reggie" Kray (October 24 1933 – October 1, 2000) Ronald and Reggie were identical twin brothers, also English criminals, the foremost perpetrators of organized crime in the East End of London during the 1950' and 1960's. With their gang called "The Firm," the Krays were involved in and accused of murder, armed robbery, arson, rackets and assaults.

3. Arthur Thompson, known as "the Godfather," was a Scottish gangster who was active in Scotland in the 1950s. He then went on to take charge of organized crime for over thirty years. He was born in September 1931 in the industrial area of Springburn, Glasgow.

4. The Clermont Club was located at 44 Berkeley Square in London's fashionable Mayfair District, and was founded by John Aspinall in 1962. The original club membership included five dukes, five marques, twenty earls, and two cabinet ministers. The Clermont set was an exclusive group of rich British gamblers who would regularly meet at the Clermont Club. What happened at the Clermont Club stayed at the Clermont Club, or at least that's what they hoped. The club closed in March 2018

5. Lord Boothby was a conservative politician that was a subject of gossip and rumors because of his overt sexuality as bisexual and his behavior. He was a supporter of homosexual law reform, though claimed he was not a homosexual. He made a comment in public that a 'sub-conscious bi-sexuality" is a component in all males and that a majority of males go through a period of exploring homosexual activity. Both the Conservatives and Labour parties kept the scandal under wraps as

was a regular guest, with his chauffer Leslie Holt[6] always there by his side. "Holt was a guy of questionable character, but very good-looking," said Brian. Rumor spread; he was a wild and gay lad. There were suspicions he and Lord Boothby were lovers. Lord Boothby wasn't new to gossip, with word spread about an alleged affair with the former Prime Minister-Harold Macmillan's wife. The only person that knew where his sexual preferences lay was Lord Boothby. Even more scandalous were rumors that Ronnie Kray and Lord Boothby both frequented gay orgies with young boys in attendance.

Larry wasn't shocked by those comments; on the other hand, hearing all of those details was very concerning. Brian saw the twins regularly at private clubs. The gay clique was relatively small and intimate in those days. Ronnie Kray was open about his sexual interests and held his male escorts close by his side. The "velvet mafia" could be rough and downright deadly if needed. One had to be careful for fear of being busted, blackmailed, or becoming removed from "normal" society living. For many tortured souls, it would be devastating. So the "velvet mafia" took control of their weakness and used it for their benefit. Explaining more about the rumored "affair" between Lord Boothby and his chauffer, Brian said that British tabloids accused Leslie Holt of being a cat burglar. Of a certainty, though, Holt was responsible for introducing Lord Boothby to the infamous Kray twins. Allegedly, the Krays supplied Boothby with young boys by way of arranged orgies, some held at Cedra Court, and in return, Boothby granted the Krays many favors. Larry's interests were peaked upon hearing all the wild stories that came from Brian. What a wild and crazy lifestyle!

When Boothby's underworld associations were revealed in England's *Sunday Express* newspaper, the conservative paper opted not to publish anything about the damaging story. The same stories about Boothby and his private life came out again by way of articles in the labor-supporting *Sunday Mirror* tabloid. Gossip had exploded everywhere with all sorts of accusations. Brian repeated that he didn't want to be involved with that gossip. Still, he was deeply troubled with his attendance at some of those parties and the interest the Krays had shown in Brian's private life.

Our research identified alleged accusations that MI5 hid for more than 50 years. MI5, it is the U.K. Security Services. The MI stands for "Military Intelligence," and there are various 'MI' branches, with 5 and 6 office

---

best they could.
6. Leslie Holt was born in 1937 in Shoreditch, England. He was a known cat burglar and a former boxer that had associations with the Kray twins. He was supposedly Conservative Party - Lord Boothby's lover and was his chauffeur.

eventually becoming the Security Service and Secret Intelligence Service (SIS). MI5 is the United Kingdom's domestic counter-intelligence and security agency and is part of its intelligence machinery alongside the Secret Intelligence Service, Government Communications Headquarters, and Defense Intelligence. And yes, that agency is very particular on what information they release to the public and how data is disseminated.

Also alleged and reported in 2015 by way of the *Telegraph*, a U.K. newspaper, was a buzz swirling around Lord Boothby and his escapades that prompted fears of Government problems. There were accusations made that he and the Krays colluded in trafficking young boys for sex. Since Brian was obviously in a mood to talk, Larry stayed on the line with an eager ear, ready and willing to hear it all. Brian worried about the gambling debt he ran up from playing Chemin de Fer, which is the game of Baccarat. It was difficult to comprehend why he lost so much money when he was good at playing that game. The thought crossed his mind that perhaps games were rigged against him.

Brian wondered what the odds of coincidence were that one of the Kray brothers always appeared right next to him at the table to express sympathy for the loss of large sums of money. He mused over how they could have known in advance. Larry thought about that for a moment and agreed with Brian's concerns. It could be part of a plot to destroy Brian in some way. Added to his fears, he was either loaded or drinking heavily, and the Krays used that as reasoning for his bad luck. One thing for sure, Larry was entirely convinced that hanging around the Kray twins wasn't a good idea.

The types of people Brian had swirling around him amazed but also concerned Larry. He thought that Brian walked down a dangerous path. Larry asked Brian if he wanted him to jump on a plane to England so he could be nearby and help him. Brian paused for a moment and replied. "Maybe we can make that happen another time, but not right now. I have to get things in order around here and need my space. I don't want to drag you into anything harmful. That genuinely disappointed Larry to hear, and if he had it to do all over again, he would have just jumped on a plane and shown up at Brian's door. But in hindsight, no one had a crystal ball to see what was around the next corner.

CHAPTER TWENTY-SIX

DIZ STRIKES A MORTAL BLOW

T he Beatles Tour started in America on August 15, 1965, and would keep Brian busy managing the hundreds of details of the tour until it ended on August 31 at San Francisco's Cow Palace. Arriving in New York City, Brian checked himself and the boys in at the Warwick Hotel and grabbed a much-needed nap. The first show was at Shea Stadium and would go down in history as the highest concert attendance in America until 1973.

Upon awakening, Brian decided to give Larry a call before he dove into his crazy work schedule. Larry's roommate Jerry answered the phone and told Brian he would relay a message to Larry as soon as he got home, reassuring Brian he would be thrilled to hear from him. Before he gave his private telephone number for Larry to reach him at, Brian mentioned he was calling from New York with an emphasis on the time difference.

An hour passed by before Larry returned home, and upon receiving the message, he didn't hesitate to return the call immediately. Brian answered with a happy sounding voice, and Larry greeted him with an uplifting attitude. Forgetting for a moment that Brian was in New York, Larry suggested they get together after the show. Realizing that was impossible, Larry let out a long sigh. Brian said he had little time to talk and profusely apologized, but he needed to head out for a dinner meeting with his attorney Nat Weiss. He told Larry that Diz would be joining them at dinner. "Diz! I thought you guys stopped seeing each other?" retorted Larry.

Brian insisted that Diz had changed his ways. He explained that even Nat was skeptical about Diz having changed for the better, but was willing to give him another chance. Larry couldn't believe what he was hearing, and sarcastically said, "You mean like a leopard can change its spots?"

When Nat Weiss first met Diz in New York with Brian, he had accompanied him to a short and brief meeting. Nat was aware of their volatile relationship and knew Diz could act out violently, attempting to hurt and humiliate Brian. He worried it could carry over into his business world and leak to the public by way of gossip, but Brian wouldn't listen to anyone when it came to his relationship with Diz. He wanted to be in control and knew what was best for him or not. Indeed, it was as if Diz had cast a spell over Brian. Also, it amazed Larry that no one around Brian had the guts to speak up and protect him from that tortured relationship; at least no one that Brian had told Larry about. Larry spoke out the best he could. Sometimes Brian listened, and sometimes he didn't.

It seemed that Diz was trying to get back into Brian's life. Brian was afraid that Diz would do something to harm him or somehow embarrass the Beatles so he asked Nat Weiss to help him. Nat agreed to help. It didn't take long to locate Diz and invite him to his office for a talk. Once in the office Diz said he didn't want anything from Brian, he just wanted to see him. Nat responded by saying "you're not going to get anything from Brian and you're not going to see him either."

"Well then," Diz said, "Brian's got lots of money. If he wants me to stay away I'll need a car, then I can go away." When Brian heard this, he ordered Nat to give Diz $3,000 to buy a car. But there was no assurance that Diz would leave right away so the deal was that Diz allow Nat to lock Diz in a hotel room at the Warwick Hotel with a private guard hired by Nat. Diz was to stay locked in that room until Brian and the Beatles left town. They left town and Diz was released.

Brian didn't like being scolded, and as a way of skirting off the topic, he promised they would get together when he returned to California during the latter part of August. His schedule was just too jam-packed with the Beatles tour and their performance at Shea Stadium for him to pin down a date or time at that moment. He also made a promise to touch base with Larry by phone in a day or two. Their conversation ended with Larry wishing Brian and the Beatles good luck and 'break-a-leg' on the opening tour performance.

A day or two passed since he spoke with Brain, and Larry was extremely curious about how the dinner with Brian, Nat, and Diz turned out. Larry had no choice but to wait until Brian contacted him again. Finally, the call came in. Brian spoke frantically, attempting to blurt out some disturbing news about another 'horrific' Diz incident. After calming down, Brian said, "I am truly embarrassed to tell you, and before you start in Larry, you warned me many times, I know, there was another terrible incident involving Diz and his scheming ways." Brian's voice was soft and on the verge of crying.

"You mean the problem occurred during the dinner with your attorney?" Brian responded with a loud "yes," stating that Diz stole not only his briefcase but also Nat Weiss's briefcase. The tone of his voice changed to one of anger. "Diz is blackmailing me and threatens to release certain photographs to the press; the ones I had in my briefcase." Brian couldn't grasp how Diz could even think of doing such a horrible thing; especially after all he had done to help him. The photos were of Brian and others in compromising positions with young men at orgies. Brian continued, "If those ever get released to the public or the police, my career and reputation will be destroyed!" While holding back tears, he said, "Diz repeatedly called me horrible names like queer and fag. He threatened that all he had to do was expose me as a queer, and my world would be turned upside down and ruined. He's requested a large sum of money before he would return anything he took from us. He wants a car along with all sorts of financial guarantees. It's truly a scary deed in that Diz stooped so low."

He told Larry the contents of his briefcase also had contracts, a substantial amount of money, and prescription drugs. Brian had no clue what was inside Nat's briefcase; it had to be important. "This is so hard for me to deal with, I don't know what to do? Nat wanted to contact the police, but I was dead set against it. I don't want to risk any bad press. It could damage the boys."

Larry, alarmed to hear what had happened, was speechless. How pathetic that one person could be so horrible to another. But then again, there were hoodlums and murderers out there. Without thinking, Larry reminded Brian that he warned him about Diz. Clearly, that wasn't the best thing to say.

Larry's anger also stemmed from the night Diz spiked his drink and then laughed about it; but how selfish of him, this was about helping Brian.

Brian was in no mood to accept any blame. Larry suggested that perhaps his roommate Jerry would call Diz. Brian said, "No, please, no, just keep all of this to you, please!"

Nat Weiss, on the other hand, wanted both briefcases with all belongings returned and hired a private detective. Nat was not about to let a criminal like Diz bully him or Brian. The hired detective was successful in tracking down Diz, who had flown back to Los Angeles. He was able to get both briefcases back after some negotiations.

There was a problem, though. Some contents from Brian's briefcase were missing. Most of the money, the drugs, and all of the sexually explicit photographs were gone. It was at that moment, severe depression set in for Brian, and it became worse over time.

Larry noticed a change in Brian after he revealed the details. He felt sad for Brian being dragged down by Diz. To console Brian, he said he would always be available, a shoulder for him to lean and cry on, happy to help by listening, and provide as much guidance as he could through the tunnels of pain.

Brian treasured Larry's kind words and support. It didn't click in his head that he needed to leave Diz alone forever. Even with all the theft, threats, blackmail, and hurt, Brian still desired a love and sex relationship with Diz. He was obsessed and possessed by Diz. There was nothing Larry or anyone else could do. Unfortunately, the relationship with Diz was based on abuse. Diz lured Brian into a morbid web of dishonesty to those that cared for him. The rough sex he craved had led Brian down into a dark world.

CHAPTER TWENTY-SEVEN

BLACKMAIL

B rian and Larry had not spoken to each other for almost a year. For no particular reason, distance, work, and Diz got in the way. During that time, Brian was consumed with keeping his empire and life on track, and Larry was promoting a band named The Game[1] signed by Nik Venet and produced by Max Hoch and Capitol Records. There were four young men in the group. George, Hans, Paul and Nanuck. He and the group's manager came up with an idea to dress the group in mini-skirts. Larry knew a great designer named Tryntje Baum, a swimsuit designer for Cole of California. Larry contacted her while she was living at the Chateau Marmot Hotel[2] on the Sunset Strip and asked her to design the group's wardrobe. She came up with a wonderful design for their new image. Years later, Tryntje married jazz flutists Paul Horn and they retired comfortably on their island in Canada.

Unfortunately, Capitol Records released the group from their label after conflicts with their producer and with the group wanting to go after a better deal. Larry and the group's manager tried to get Rick Jarrard, a record producer at RCA, to sign the group. At the same time, a press package was sent to the Ed Sullivan Show. The Sullivan production office was stunned when they saw photos of the band in formal mini-skirt suits. Liking what they saw, the production group responded that if "The Game" could get a

THE GAIM

record deal, they would be happy to arrange an appearance on the show. All Larry needed to do was sign the group to a new record label. Capitol Records owned the name "The Game" so they had to change their name to "The Gaim" for legal reasons. As luck would have it, or rather lack of, RCA didn't sign the act. Over the next

1. The Gaim/The Game – George Leovy - rhythm guitar, Hans Ahlert – Bass Guitar, Paul Nussbaum – lead guitar, George "Nanuck" Byrnes – Drums
2. Chateau Marmont is located at 8221 Sunset Boulevard in Los Angeles on the Sunset Strip. It was built in 1929. It was modeled after the Chateau d'Amboise a royal retreat in France's Loire Valley. Currently the hotel has 63 rooms and suites and is a seven story L-shaped building.

several months, all other attempts for a new record label failed. Eventually, the group disbanded, in part due to the Vietnam War draft.

Needing to keep a roof over his head and cover his living expenses, Larry concentrated on making money. He no longer drove a taxi because his attempts at record promoting, producing, and working as a personal manager took up most of his time. Larry also juggled another job as an engineer at a recording studio in Hollywood, a place called DCT Recording.[3] Somehow he managed to fit selling cars part-time into his busy schedule.

Larry tapped into inspirations gained from Brian and worked for similar success. Wishful thinking kept his spirits up. Fond thoughts about Brian were always in his heart, and he sensed that one day they would reconnect. Sad thoughts also crept in, remembering the last time they communicated; Brian was being eaten alive by threats and blackmail. He suspected Diz played a significant role in keeping them from talking with each other. Perhaps Brian was upset because Larry told him not to be involved with Diz. He knew that created friction between the two of them. Wondering why they lost touch, it's funny that he didn't pick up the phone to call him. Of course, that went both ways, Brian had his share of business activities, keeping him busy. What Larry didn't know was that some health issues and more troubles were affecting Brian's life.

One evening, after he got home from the recording studio out of the blue and to his great surprise, Larry received an overseas phone call. Brian softly said, "Hey, stranger! How are you doing? We haven't talked for such a long time. I've missed you." Larry was so surprised and overjoyed to hear from Brian that he stumbled for words. He hoped Brian was having better luck with relationships.

Brian started by telling Larry that Lonnie left his employment. It was upsetting to hear, but Lonnie's departure was inevitable; there were consequences to not treating a friend right. With Lonnie gone, the task of finding another valet to attend to his flat and personal needs was a high priority. Brian was lucky to find a highly recommended replacement named Antonio. Along with his wife Maria, they lived in an extra room in Brian's flat. It was a perfect arrangement for both Brian and the couple. Antonio's mastery of the English language was minimal, but enough to do the job. Brian realized that it was a good idea to have someone "straight" handling the household matters.

3. DCT Recording Studios was located at 6414 Sunset Blvd. Hollywood California 90028. It was owned by Frank Waring and a mastering / recording studio. It became famous for mastering artists Steppenwolf, Buffalo Springfield, Iron Butterfly and Three Dog Night.

On the business front, Brian said that a man by the name of Robert Stigwood[4] wanted to merge his business with NEMS. He also wanted to take ownership of the Beatles. Brian didn't mind a potential business venture between NEMS and Stigwood, but he didn't want to give up control of the Beatles. On top of that, the infamous Kray brothers were blackmailing Brian for money since they couldn't secure a part of the Beatles Empire. Rumors circulated that Stigwood initially offered to buy NEMS, but the arrangement eventually turned into a merger.

The business transaction would be beneficial for Stigwood and would have successfully placed him at the peak of the British pop industry. Epstein was the only person at NEMS who was keen on the Stigwood-NEMS merger because of financial stability. Alastair Taylor is reported to have said, "You must be joking!" when Brian told him of the merger under consideration. Under duress, Epstein considered handing over his role as manager of the Beatles. When the Fab Four learned of that possibility, they were outraged. Evidently, they disliked Stigwood with a passion. Interviewed in 2000 by Greil Marcus, Paul McCartney recalled the group's angry reaction: "We said, In fact, if you do somehow manage to pull this off, we promise you one thing. We will record God Save the Queen for every single record we make from now on, and we'll sing it out of tune. That's a promise. So if this guy buys us that is what he'll buy."

There was a rumor that Stigwood and the Kray brothers were working together, which added another layer of paranoia to Brian's life. Brian's world was starting to fall apart, and it didn't go unnoticed. People grabbed at him from all directions hoping to take advantage while he was so vulnerable. Larry jokingly said to Brian, "See what happens when we stop keeping in touch with each other! I told you I should have come to England to rescue you, but you wouldn't have it at the time." Whether in poor taste or not, Larry couldn't help letting Brian know how he felt. Even hearing about Brian's problems, the entire conversation was enjoyable, and Larry was grateful he called.

A few more months passed without the two of them talking. Why there was silence bothered Larry with each passing day. An increased amount of drugs and alcohol consumption could very well be a contributing factor. It was evident from their last conversation that depression and extreme

---

4. Robert Colin Stigwood was born on April 16, 1934 and died January 4, 2016. He was an Australian born British resident music entrepreneur, film producer and promoter. He is best known for managing Cream and the Bee Gees and theatrical productions like Hair and Jesus Christ Superstar, and film productions including the extremely successful movies Grease and Saturday Night Fever.

mood swings could make it harder for Brian to focus his attention. On many occasions, Larry wanted to pick up the phone and call him, but he didn't. To this day, it bothers Larry that he didn't.

CHAPTER TWENTY-EIGHT

THE POINT OF BREAKING

Larry basked in another beautiful sunny California day filled with work and mingling with friends. Enjoyment came from the type of work he was now involved in at the recording studio in Hollywood. But, the longer work schedules kept him worn out, and the late nights meant he slept later than usual.

The telephone rang, waking Larry from a deep, dreamy sleep. It was Brian's voice on the other end, and he didn't sound very good. Larry shook his head back and forth a few times trying to wake up. Hearing Brian's voice made his heart quiver, but worry set in at the same time. Once again, Brian sounded beat up, not in the literal sense, but emotionally. He was worn out and hadn't slept well for weeks. He seemed on the verge of emotional and physical collapse and talked in a slow whisper into the phone. After some cordial greeting exchanges, he told Larry he would be leaving London for a few days for a much-needed vacation to his country home in Warbleton, Sussex.

It was evident by the tone of his voice that he needed some rest. Larry gently responded, "From the way you sound, Brian, I do think it's a good idea you get away from it all. You sound stressed out, and that isn't good for your physical or mental health. Are you sure you can safely drive? I'm really worried about you."

"I know you are Larry, and I thank you from the depths of my heart. I also know you've always been honest with me, and I do need the rest. I feel so beat up, tired, and lonely. Most people see me on top of the world because I manage the greatest group in the world. But, I am not a Beatle. I don't get any recognition for my contributions to their success. Yes, they write the songs and have the talent, but I take all that talent to the next level for the world to notice, hear, and enjoy. I'm not trying to be an egotist, but I am trying to make you realize how terribly lonely I feel being left aside in the wings. And it appears there isn't a person out there that isn't trying to use me for one thing or another."

"When it comes to the Beatles, there are four of them, and they can bounce off each other whenever they have a problem. Larry, you probably are the only one I can truly share my problems with, but you aren't here. There are times I feel such hollowness in my chest. All I want is to love and be loved in return. I know you love me, Larry, but the relationship we have isn't the same as it is with Diz. I can't get the desires I have for him out of my mind! Diz is always in my thoughts, like a tape machine going round and round in my head. It's maddening! I need to escape for a while, to take a vacation from it all." Brian explained it was the Bank Holiday and a perfect time for families and just about everyone to escape. Therefore, no one would question his leaving town and it won't be considered odd for him to disappear for a few days.

The eighteenth-century country home was Brian's retreat from the craziness of business life and a beautiful drive of only fifty miles from his flat in London. That home was Brian's retreat from the madness of business life. Arrangements were made for Peter Brown and Geoffrey Ellis to join him for the holiday. He wouldn't be alone but with old and close friends. Brian kept another love interest nearby, but his true desires remained for Diz and the hopes he would join him. Perhaps time away would be the much-needed healing for the problems of late.

Hearing Diz's name was annoying and disappointing. After the briefcase incident, it was hard to believe Brian would even allow Diz back into his life. He wondered if Diz was going back and forth between the United States and England, and if so, certainly on Brian's dime. Damn it, he thought to himself. It was apparent Brian couldn't learn his lesson. It's the true definition of insanity, Brian expecting a different result each time. In the past, Larry wondered if Brian was on a collision course, to self-destruction, but now he realized Brian was headed straight towards a catastrophe of hurt. He believed Diz was deliberately manipulating Brian's emotions, to the point of breaking. Diz was in full control. Hearing all of Brian's troubles hurt Larry deeply. Here was a man he cared so much for, suffering terribly.

Initially, Diz told Brian he would join him at his country home. Then he called to say he had other plans and wouldn't join him after all. He did that several times. The going back and forth, changing his mind, was driving Brian mad with anxiety. After realizing times were harder than he could have imagined, Larry wished he could be in England to help Brian. It was a mute topic and no point in bringing it up. All things considered, distance proved to be the best solution.

The conversation between them lasted longer than Larry had time for; he had an appointment and couldn't be late for it. It was necessary to inform Brian they would need to talk later so he could get to his meeting. Later on, as the years passed, Larry regretted having to end that conversation when he did.

CHAPTER TWENTY-NINE

BYE BYE LUV

Later that same evening, Brian called again. He began by telling Larry he drove out to the country house looking forward to some holiday fun and relaxation. His hopes for Diz to make a showing were shattered. While that wasn't the first thing Larry wanted to hear, he was relieved to hear from Brian so soon after having to cut their prior talk short.

Brian explained that he became more depressed after Diz called him at the country house to say he wouldn't be there, flaunting the excuse of a big party he was going to attend in London. A few hours after that telephone call, Brian turned very edgy about being out in the country. His feeling of loneliness and lack of companionship got to him. He decided to leave the country and go back to his home on Chapel Street. Brian thought about and surely convinced himself that Diz would show up after the party. Diz would be more comfortable with it being just the two of them together rather than being with other people at the country house.

When Brian arrived back home, he found no one was there to greet him but wasn't surprised. He thought Antonio and Maria must have gone to visit their relatives for the long weekend. Even his business secretary hadn't planned on being at the house. Brian had invited her to the country, but she already had other plans.

According to Brian, Antonio, and his wife, Maria, kept to themselves when not performing the tasks required of them. They had not intended to spend the entire weekend away from responsibilities. When they returned to Brian's flat, they saw Brian's car parked outside. Believing that Brian had returned early from his trip, they left him to his privacy, not wanting to bother him. They were confident if he needed something they would hear from him.

That particular Friday night would be a long one for Brian. He had swallowed a couple of pills in attempts to feel better and soothe his heartache. Brian told Larry he attempted to contact Simon Napier-Bell a few times earlier that evening, but he didn't answer the phone, so he left a few messages. Larry didn't understand why Brian was telling him all of this now, but he encouraged him to keep talking. Since Larry couldn't be there in person, this was the next best thing.

Brian also mentioned he called Peter Brown before calling Larry. Peter told him he sounded groggy, but Brian only admitted to being tired. Peter was happy to know Brian made it home safely from the country, but Brian told Larry he seemed to be making a fuss over him. To help Brian relax, Larry recommended he get a good night's sleep and expressed that tomorrow, hopefully, would be a better day. He said, "Your mind should be clearer after some needed rest while allowing the pills you took to wear off and get out of your system. Please, Brian, go to sleep now. We can talk more over the weekend or any time you want, give me a call. But please promise me you will go to sleep." Brian promised and then mumbled a good-bye luv and hung up the telephone.

CHAPTER THIRTY

WITNESS TO MURDER

The next day Larry received another phone call from Brian. He remembered the phone kept ringing and ringing and ringing. He was sleeping at the time and thought the sound was part of a dream. While it was early in the middle of the afternoon for Larry, it was late in the evening for Brian. Larry finally woke up enough to answer the telephone before it stopped ringing. Brian's voice sounded like he had never gone to sleep; he sounded weak and desperate.

Before Larry could ask any questions, Brian mentioned that what Robert Stigwood wanted in a partnership was more than Brian could let him have. That was very upsetting, even though in public, he tried to show he was for the merger. But why would Brian want to give up half his business interests when he was doing so well? It couldn't all be for financial gains. On top of that, the Kray twins were backing Stigwood, and that type of sponsorship scared Brian to death.

Some evil characters were infiltrating his life, and that wasn't good, no matter how you looked at it. During their exchange, it was hard at times for Larry to understand the words Brian said. He thought the problem might be due to the transatlantic connection not being clear, but more and more, he felt that Brian was under the influence of heavy drugs. Brian wouldn't admit to taking any, but Larry doubted that.

Throughout all of this, Brian continued to confide in Larry in ways that went beyond what they had shared in the past. He kept telling Larry how much he loved Diz as if saying it would make Diz love Brian the same way. He also said he loved Larry but in a different way. His two loves were very different; one was about trust and caring; the other was about mistrust, and deception, abuse, and torture.

Larry was touched when Brian said he loved him, but to hear Brian say he loved Diz made Larry sick. One would think the pain and anguish caused by Diz would destroy some of that love, but it wasn't the case. Brian had many other sex partners, but the only person he wanted to have a meaningful relationship with, regardless of the fact it was destroying him, was with 'Diz' Gillespie. Larry felt a knot in his stomach. It was too painful and upsetting to hear Brian suffering so.

Having managed to carry the telephone with him over to the kitchen, he made himself a cup of coffee while Brian went on to say that Diz called in a panic a few months back. Yes, there was yet another Diz story to be told! Larry made his cup of coffee, and went over to the couch to sit down, ready to hear more about Diz.

"One night, while in a pub having a beer, Diz witnessed a murder."

"Murder?" Larry stood up in disbelief as he listened carefully to each word Brian said.

When Diz called Brian at home that night, he had no idea Diz was even in England. As long as Brian continued to give him money and supply his habits, Diz went back and forth between the two countries. So hearing him sounding hysterical came as a shock.

When Diz arrived back in London, he went to a pub called "The Blind Beggar"[1] for a few drinks. Supposedly he was alone at the time, nursing a beer. The pub was located on Whitechapel Road in Whitechapel, in the east end of London. Why Diz decided to go there was never made clear. Diz was sitting at a table enjoying his drink when Ronnie Kray walked in and without warning walked right up to a man, later reported as George Cornell, and shot him dead right in the forehead. Then Ronnie turned around and walked out as quickly as he had entered. There was no guilt or emotion from Ronnie, only anger and hatred in his eyes.

Scared out of his wits, Diz felt his muscles tighten as his body prepared for flight or fight. He had witnessed a killing, not just any killing, but a murder committed by Ronnie Kray, and that put him in an extremely dangerous position. His heart was racing in a state of paranoia and panic. During the commotion, he slipped out the backdoor before anyone noticed. That frightened Brian as well. The Kray brothers had

---

1. The Blind Beggar is a pub on Whitechapel Road in Whitechapel in the East of London, England. It is where Ronnie Kray murdered George Cornell in front of witnesses. It is the location of William Booth's first sermon, which led to the creation of the Salvation Army. It was the nearest outlet for the Mann's Albion brewery, where the first modern Brown Ale was brewed. The pub was built in 1894 on the site of an inn that had been established before 1654, and takes it's name from the legend of Henry de Montfort F. El.337 Whitechapel Road, London E1 1BU, England.

become even more powerful in recent months and were considered dangerous men. If they found out Diz witnessed the murder, all hell would break loose for Brian.

Once again, he brought up that past encounter when he ran into the Krays at a social event in a club called "Esmeralda's Barn." The club had since closed, but it was a club they owned. Brian believed all the rumors about the Kray brothers. On another outing, the Kray twins walked up to Brian and formally met Diz. Brian knew that both he and Diz were familiar faces to the Krays, and that was very disturbing. Larry felt beads of sweat forming on his forehead. Brian knew it would only be a matter of time before he heard from Ronnie or Reggie Kray. For that matter, he was afraid he might hear from Scotland Yard because of his association with Diz. A murder investigation would take place.

Just as Brian had predicted, Reggie approached him at a club and told him he knew all about his little escapades with his "boy-toy Diz." He said if he didn't keep Diz's mouth shut, he would bring a lot of trouble to Brian and possibly, the Beatles. Since the Krays were sociopathic killers and had no scruples, the threat was a serious matter. Reggie also mentioned that he had compromising photos of Brian that he received from Diz. A shock wave went through Brian's body! It shocked Brian so much that he wasn't even sure he heard him correctly. It could have been a bluff tactic just to blackmail him. If it was true, then the photos were the ones in the briefcase that Diz stole in New York. Sex photos in the hands of the Kray twins made Brian's heart stop beating. He could only assume the worst-case scenario. He told Reggie as calmly as he could, not to worry, Diz would keep quiet. But honestly, Brian had no idea how he would accomplish that; Diz was a man out only for himself.

Added to these fears were more blackmail threats from Diz. Blackmail was just one of the "tools" in Diz's bag of horrors. Reggie Kray backed off after that, allowing Brian to catch his breath, but Diz became more of a problem every day. Brian explained that Diz was an emotional wreck, and a crazed Diz was a dangerous Diz! He left the pub quickly, running out the back door as fast as he could, with no destination in mind. It was amazing no one outside saw him running like a crazy man. He hailed a taxicab at the end of the street and told the driver to drop him off at a location he would point out. Diz was within two blocks from Brian's home.

He said to Brian that no one realized he was even at the club at the time of the murder. With the sound of the gunshot and seeing the blood, it was too chaotic for anyone to notice Diz. However there was a lady bartender who served Diz his beer, but Diz hardly spoke to her. She wouldn't have known if he was still there or had gone by the time Ronnie walked in. Regardless, it was terrifying to have witnessed such cold brutality. With news of the murder spreading rapidly, Scotland Yard would be looking for witnesses.

Ironically, it made Brian feel special that the first call Diz made while in a state of panic was to him. The tables had turned, and now Diz was the one asking for help. It made Brian feel needed, a feeling he had not felt from Diz before.

Unfolding at the same time and unbeknownst to Brian or Larry, Scotland Yard and MI5 were monitoring Lord Boothby on his unusual affairs. All investigations resulted in denials, but the topic became controversial. It was rumored that Scotland Yard had photos of gay orgies that allegedly took place at Boothby's flat. A lot of powerful men could have been cornered and questioned or even blackmailed. Was the timing just a coincidence or not? Brian worried that some of those photos might have images of him. The pressure, fear, and insecurity that Brian was experiencing were too much, so he sank deeper into drugs, alcohol, and Diz. Brian was totally alone in this. There was no one he could turn to; no one to help him except Larry, and all he could do was listen as a friend.

What didn't cross Brian's mind initially, as he explained to Larry, was that word came by way of an anonymous tip that Diz might be an informant for Scotland Yard or the FBI. It certainly was possible. If it was true, Diz could be excused for all his criminal deeds, arrest records, and contributions to the underworld. He quivered with that thought. How could any person become even worse than he already was? How could Diz do such things to him? Diz, the man he loved and desired to be by his side. The thoughts whirling around in his head really blew Brian's mind. It's as if Diz was a Svengali, manipulating and using his powers over Brian to keep him spellbound and weak. Brian was a junkie, and Diz was the drug.

It crossed Brian's mind many times that Scotland Yard might have some, if not all, the photographs that were stolen. He told Larry he never got a straight answer from Diz as to what happened to those photographs. Since their disappearance, Brian felt like he had an open wound of ulcers due to worry. Larry thought about Charles Schultz, the creator of the comic characters "Peanuts." Larry envisioned Lucy pulling the football away from Charlie Brown after promising she wouldn't. Yet time after time, over and over again, she pulled that football away from poor Charlie Brown. That's what Diz was doing to Brian.

No one could control Diz with his wild and crazy behavior. His demands for more money and drugs were unending. There was nobody more rotten to the core than Diz Gillespie.

Brian was sinking in a quicksand of fear. Fear that Diz would desert him. Fear that Scotland Yard had explicit photos, fear that the Kray twins were planning his murder, fear that his boys, the Beatles might find out, fear that his homosexuality would be discovered, fear and more fear.

LOOK UP NOT DOWN
BEATLES TODAY, WHAT TOMORROW?
no other
GODS
before
$100,000 FREE PRIZES!
WORLD

CHAPTER THIRTY-ONE

IN HELL

O bvious to Larry were Brian's moments of high anxiety and fears. He was emotional, understandably so, and continued to ramble on. At times he talked faster than his mouth could form words, which resulted in gibberish. Brian narrowed in about J. Edgar Hoover and the probing into his life. The last thing he wanted was for the Beatles or his other acts to be dragged into any scandals. Larry wondered if Brian was mistaken. The Beatles, actually John Lennon, was in hot water due to a "Jesus Christ" comparison statement he made. That comment drew the FBI's attention to Brian and the Beatles, with negative insinuations. The Beatles were so popular with most teenagers just by using the power of their music. If you stop to think about FBI investigations, who could even fathom the possibility of Lord Boothby and the Beatles being used in the same sentence together?

Larry was aware of the negative news articles on John Lennon. He picked up an international newspaper from a local newsstand and read about it in the *Evening Standard*. The article was about one of the famous Beatles comparing religion with their popularity. In the article, Lennon was quoted saying, "Christianity will go, will vanish and shrink. I don't argue about that; I know I am right, and I will be proved right. We're now more popular than Jesus. I don't know which will go first – Rock n' Roll or Christianity.

What Brian shared with Larry was mind-boggling. Larry had to stand up while scrambling for any words to say, shaking his head back and forth in skepticism. He let out a big sigh, wishing it a nightmare. How overwhelmingly wild! Rather abruptly, Brian said he had to get off the telephone so that he could use the loo (bathroom). He asked Larry to stay close to the phone so that he could call him right back. That "right back" turned out to be a long time. After waiting for about two and a half hours, Larry decided to take a shower. Wouldn't you know it, just as he was about to get into the shower, the telephone rang. It was Brian calling him back, just as he said he would, but not right after the loo visit.

Brian's speech was slurred, as if he was drunk. Humorously Larry thought he would need an interpreter. He struggled to understand Brian's response after asking him if he was okay. Finally, he was able to comprehend that Brian was saying that everything would be all right once Diz arrived. The statement shocked Larry. What did he mean? Had Diz called Brian to say he was coming over? Or was Brian delusional? What took Brian so long to call Larry back? He scratched his head in bewilderment. Brian acted like a teenager whose first love was cheating on him, forever lamenting a broken heart. In an instant, their exchange became a bizarre and disturbing conversation. In a moment of opening up his soul, Brian randomly said he had been admitted to the Priory Hospital in Roehampton London last year due to a prescription drug overdose. In time Larry found out that the priory hospital was a mental hospital and concluded that Brian must have been trying to deal with his demons and had a breakdown.

The fact Brian admitted his hospitalization to Larry was surprising to hear. He was such a proper man, and confessing such a medical problem was an indication of a man severely beaten down. Larry felt the pain coming from Brian's broken voice and also felt a sense of importance that he shared it with him. It was therapeutic for Brian to talk about this particularly dark episode in his life. Faithfully he continued to listen with hopes that Brian's opening up would help him get out of that moment of depression he was experiencing. With his whole heart, he wanted Brian to have the world at his feet in business success and personal happiness. It weighed heavily on his soul that Brian had become so insecure and unable to focus on his own wellbeing.

He wasn't able to enjoy happiness the way he deserved.

Game playing was an evil way for Diz to find a place in Brian's heart. Diz didn't care about anyone but himself. If Diz even knew that Brian confided in Larry, he would make life more difficult. How many times does betrayal and hurt from a person need to happen before the reality sets in that it isn't worth the pain any longer? It's a very sad but true story, afflicting many people looking for the right person. Being gay added another level of difficulty. Those looking for love in all the wrong places are the ones most gullible to the works of dishonesty from sociopathic people with a destructive nature. From Larry's point of view, it was always amazing how Brian managed to keep so much of his life secret and hidden from those that appeared close to him. He had fallen so deep into the rabbit hole that he remained held down by the claws of a desperately unfulfilled love.

It was a perfect storm for a disaster that included the use of drugs and alcohol. Larry thought there had to be someone else in Brian's life that was close enough to him in London, close enough, and trusted at some level. However, Brian never revealed to Larry who those persons could be, or if anyone even existed. Multiple times Larry offered to go to Brian in England, and each time an excuse was given as to why the timing wasn't right. Brian's world had spun out of control. Like the children's nursery rhyme, Brian had fallen from the wall, but there were no King's men to put him back together again. Brian was in Hell.

CHAPTER THIRTY-TWO

THE LAST PERSON TO SEE BRIAN ALIVE

Larry determined Brian was hitting rock bottom from lack of sleep in addition to his indulgence of pills and alcohol. He knew Brian could hold his own, but when too much was too much he wasn't in a position to measure. Larry believed that if Brian got a good night's sleep, he would wake up the next day feeling much better, ready to take on another day. He hoped Brian would remember their lengthy phone chat because it had been so very revealing, sensitive, truthful, and therapeutic. But, drugs, alcohol, and lack of sleep can alter the memory, as we all know.

Without really thinking it through entirely, Larry blurted out, "Since you're worried about investigations, do you think either Scotland Yard or the FBI would tap your phone?" Brian quickly said, "Hold on for a moment." Larry heard Brian call out " Is someone there?" In the momentary silence, Larry heard muffled sounds as though Brian was holding his hand over the receiver. Although unclear, it sounded like Brian was talking to someone in the room. Larry wasn't sure what was happening. And then he heard Brian gasp and say, "Oh my God," and at that moment, Larry was sure he heard another voice in the room. It was too far in the background to recognize who it was or what was being said. Suddenly the phone went silent.

Did the connection drop? Could Brian have hung up the phone? Did Scotland Yard or the FBI tap into their conversation? There was a moment of shock by what had just happened, not sure what to do or think. Larry scratched his head in bewilderment before trying to call Brian back, not only once but several times.

At first, he could not get a connection through the overseas operator. Once he got a connection, Brian wasn't answering his phone. That was the very last time Larry spoke to Brian.

Questions kept spinning around in Larry's head about what he heard right before the phone line went dead. Larry wasn't high and hadn't had anything to drink, even the night before. It was a bit overwhelming because he tried to recall to a moment whatever it was he heard in the background. He tried hard to remember, and while there were moments of silence during their conversation, was there anything else he heard that could complete this puzzle?

Could it be that Diz had just arrived and walked into Brian's room while he and Larry were on the phone? After all, that's the only person Brian was expecting and wanted to arrive. Perhaps that expectation was just wishful thinking. Was his phone tapped, and the call mysteriously ended by Scotland Yard or the FBI? Was it his resident butler Antonio that walked in, embarrassing Brian? Larry kept brainstorming, trying to come up with possibilities.

There was another voice Larry heard in the background and, he became surer of it with each passing moment. Larry took a logical approach when thinking about it, realizing the domestic help wouldn't just walk in without knocking first. He continued to question himself about what he heard in Brian's bedroom. Speaking out loud, he said, "It sure sounded like it was Diz's voice in the background! That voice sounded too familiar to ignore, just like a recalled terror that struck a nerve from the past." He was practically certain that mystery voice belonged to John 'Diz' Gillespie; that cocky voice was embedded forever in his memory banks.

But what if Brian was greeting another person, a new lover that could enter his house and bedroom, someone else he had given the keys to? But in opposing that thought, how would anyone get inside without the domestic help, not knowing about it. They would hear keys and a door opening and shutting. Maybe it was someone they recognized and therefore didn't question. Or, could Diz sneak inside without Antonio and Maria hearing? He remembered Brian telling him that Diz had a key to his flat so he could come and go as he pleased, even when Brian was out of town. Larry always thought that was a big mistake. Also, if Brian had taken the key away from him, which he doubted, Diz would have made a copy and kept it secret. Larry's imagination was beginning to get wild.

Once inside the bedroom, Diz could have quickly helped himself and Brian to the endless supply of pills, knowing they would enhance their wild and rough sex together. Diz believed their relationship was all about hard sex and drugs. Of course, that included anything else he could get out of Brian. Larry knew it was possible for Diz to show up anytime and continue to play his mind games with Brian. Unless Brian had called him to say otherwise, Diz thought Brian was at his country estate for the weekend. Even with all the trouble Diz caused for him, Brian hoped that a changed Diz would eventually return and love would blossom forever. It's odd how people chase after that which they can't have.

Sadly Brian continued holding on to false and desperate hopes. Brian only wanted love and companionship and would fly dangerously close to the flames of disaster whenever he was with Diz. Each time they were together provided an opportunity to test the limits, going even further into darkness. Brian was consumed by this toxic love along with drugs, alcohol, erotic lust, and the chaos that went along with a bleeding heart. Who was that someone Larry heard Brian talk to in the last moments before the phone line went dead? To this day, it continues to haunt Larry because that person was the last to see Brian alive.

The Beatles were about four hundred miles away on the West Coast of the British Isles in Bangor on the north coast of Wales. They were attending a Transcendental Meditation Seminar with the Maharishi Mahesh Yogi[1] when Brian was found dead on Sunday night, August 27th, 1967, at the young age of 32 years old. He was found alone inside his bedroom, with the curtains drawn, an eerie feeling and aroma in the air, and only a slight breeze blowing through an opened bedroom window.

The devastating news of Brian Epstein's death reached Larry in the same manner as the rest of the world, with everyone becoming aware at the same time. Larry heard the heart-wrenching news over the radio while driving to the dealership he was working for at the time. Upon hearing that tragic news, he had to slow down and pull the car over to the side of the road. Larry sat there in shock as if a bolt of lightning had penetrated his entire body and soul. Thinking his ears might have been playing tricks on him, he turned the radio dial to find another news channel. The terrible news was repeated over and over again, blasted over the airwaves no matter which channel he tuned in. The thought of their last conversation and how it ended had continually bothered him, and now this! How did this happen and who is responsible? Tears streamed down Larry's eyes.

The news reported many prescription pill bottles sat on the nightstand next to Brian's bedside. Reports also stated that all prescription bottles were tightly closed and neatly positioned. As neat and tidy as Brian was known to be, Larry wondered how someone so "out of it" on liquor and pills could have kept everything so neat and tidy? Perhaps not an impossible task for someone so meticulous as Brian was.

1. Maharishi Mahesh Yogi was an Indian guru, born January 12, 1917 in Panduka area of Raipur India. He was a disciple and assistant to Swami Brahmanda Saraswati the spiritual leader of the Himalayas. George Harrison's wife Pattie was the first to attend lectures, then brought George with her, and eventually Paul McCartney and his girlfriend Jane Asher attended talks. The Maharishi first met all the Beatles in London on August 1967.

Larry kept thinking about what he heard and concluded that maybe Diz, knowing how Brian lined up his bottles and kept orderly, placed them in neat order so to take away any suspicions. Or perhaps when his dead body was discovered, those in the room cleaned up before authorities arrived, protecting him from scandal. But they too must have wondered, how and why. There had to be more to this unfortunate event than was revealed.

Perhaps if someone had been in Brian's room manipulating the evening, they staged the overdose to appear accidental. That was something to think about. Once again, Larry had thoughts about the silence of the early morning and how easily a visitor could have left the bedroom and gone out the front door in a shadow of early morning London mist.

When Larry heard more details surrounding Brian's death, he was even more astounded – surprised because the last conversation he had with Brian had ended so abruptly.

That last conversation haunted Larry. Still digesting the tragic news of his dearest friend, he could only wonder if anything about their conversation that final night could have been a sign of something foul in the air. He felt a migraine headache pulsating in his head. Larry's entire body felt drained as if all the blood had rushed to his feet. He was exhausted from the grief, and he felt so alone. Death is such a hard thing to get one's arms around. Death at a young age for any reason is too early. One moment life is good, and you're the manager of the world's greatest Rock n' Roll band. The next moment is death. Brian died all alone … … … Or did he?

CHAPTER THIRTY-THREE

ALL HE NEEDED WAS LOVE

Feeling paralyzed, Larry couldn't do anything but sit in his car and think about it all, his mind spinning in disbelief. He had a hard time believing it. How could this have happened? Sitting in the car and crying his eyes out, there was an urgency to open the door and vomit on the curb. It just couldn't be possible. Denial.

Yet, when he thought about Brian's state of mind and how miserable he was, was it possible he could have taken his own life? Was Diz responsible? How about the Kray brothers? They had interests to gain if Brian wasn't around. Those thoughts haunted Larry. Over and over again, he questioned whether Diz was inside Brian's bedroom while Larry was on the phone with him? How he wished those thoughts didn't consume him. It's the same as trying to put logic to it and solve the mystery of why Brian died.

Was there something he should do, call someone? But whom could he call? He didn't keep any of Brian's contacts or phone numbers and felt trapped by the total isolation. Larry toiled with the idea of calling London's Scotland Yard. But what could he tell them that mattered? Calling them could put him under the spotlight. Larry just wasn't sure! Did it matter he had a conversation with Brian sometime before his death? If evidence of foul play existed, it would have come out in the news. If there were any doubts or suspicions, they would investigate. But then again, maybe there were plenty of reasons to hide the truth. The grief he felt was overwhelming.

Could Larry have made a difference? Why didn't Brain pick up the phone when he called him back after being disconnected? Larry kept visualizing Diz being there with Brian and responsible for Brian's death. He wished those thoughts would go away and stop bothering him.

Larry remembered closing his car door but had no recollection of what he did after that. Time seemed to stop. He was numb and couldn't remember if he made it to work or if he went straight home. Surely the dealership would have tried to reach him at home if he hadn't made it to work. But he wasn't at home! Larry had a vague recollection of driving up the Pacific Coast Highway to clear his mind, but it was all a blur. Thoughts were spinning around in his head, feeling like tidal waves pounding against his head.

When his head stopped pounding, and nerves settled down, he started to think of fond memories with Brian. Laughing, he wondered who else could say that Brian Epstein pushed his car to get it started? Larry knew how much Brian enjoyed it because he told him so. He kidded Larry about not fixing the car because he enjoyed being partly responsible for getting that old crummy Fiat rolling along on the road. They shared some very personal and intimate moments, many incredible gourmet dinners, and every type of emotion and feeling. That made their relationship unique, and the true definition of a caring, loving, and personal bond. Both had such a connection and closeness, one that Larry cherishes and will for the rest of his life.

When all has been said and done, Brian Epstein only craved what we all want out of life. That is true love and true friendship with a partner that gives it unconditionally. He gave the world happiness for eternity, and yet he was denied what he most needed.

CHAPTER THIRTY-FOUR

LOVE IS ALL YOU NEED

L arry sat alone in his room with expanding feelings and suspicions about Brian's death. He envisioned that on any day moving forward, he would read in a newspaper that John "Diz" Gillespie had been arrested for being involved with Brian's death. Or, perhaps he would learn that the Kray twins had something to do with Brian's death. But nothing ever transpired that validated Larry's suspicions. It's as if Brian had been murdered in part by the existing laws of that time.

It's disturbing that nothing about Diz was found, anywhere. Not one person that Larry knew had seen him since Brian's death. It's as if Diz vanished into thin air, and that only added to the mystery surrounding Brian's death. At least it does for Larry.

"Life has given me the greatest gift of being able to be a lover and a true friend to Brian Epstein. I am so grateful our paths crossed in life." Larry also reflected on and revealed for the first time, "I shared a moment in time with Brian and got to know him like so few people ever did. That we talked on the phone that last evening is heartbreaking for me, but cherished at the same time. Brian will remain in my heart and soul forever. It might have been pleasantly different if only I could have gone with Brian to the Bahamas when the Beatles were filming *HELP*. I think it would have changed both of our lives tremendously."

"The last time I heard Brian's voice, sounding so desperate and sad, has been very difficult for me, difficult because I couldn't be in the same room to help Brian get over the emotional pain he was having. How wonderfully fulfilled his life could have been without Diz in his life. I really cared for and loved Brian and he knew it. But Brian thought he was in love with Diz, at least in a way he believed love should be." I had to respect his passions.

"Now it is essential I open up and tell this story. Brian was a brilliant, smart, and gifted person with a great eye for talent. On a personal note, after all, what Brian wanted was a relationship with a person he loved, and a person that would love him reciprocally in the same way. Brian just wanted to be accepted and loved for the person he was, and not for his celebrity or money. He didn't get the love or recognition he so deserved."

As the saying goes, love is what makes the world go round, and Brian wanted to be part of that world.

Was Brian depressed enough to commit suicide? Sadly, it almost happened before. During the Beatle's final tour of the U.S., Brian's mood swings were deeply troubling to those close to him. The Beatles had told him that they no longer would tour. While still in L.A. with one more show in San Francisco, Brian announced that Diz had traveled to L.A. to see him, and they would be getting together in just a few hours. Nat Weiss was there and angrily told Brian that he must not have anything to do with that horrible young man. Brian dismissed Nat saying that Diz loved him.

After spending the day and night together in a rented house without incident, Diz got up early and went to the bungalow at the Beverly Hills Hotel to retrieve his suitcase. When Nat and Brian showed up, Diz was gone, and so were their briefcases. Brian became deeply depressed, so Peter Brown agreed to stay with him at Chapel Street for a few days. One night after dinner, Brian went to his room and went to sleep. Peter checked on him several times, but when he noticed that Brian had not changed his position, he tried to wake him up without success. He was out cold, and slapping him didn't bring him around.

Peter called Dr. Cowan, and they took Brian to the hospital where he had his stomach pumped. When he woke up, he told Peter that it had been a foolish accident and he didn't mean to do it. But later, when Peter returned to Chapel Street, he found a suicide note next to an empty bottle of pills on the nightstand next to Brian's bed.

In a letter written to Nat Weiss just three days before he died, Brian said, "Eric's album makes lovely happy, contented dreamy listening. I am very addicted to Anderson. Till the second, love, flowers, bells, be happy, and look forward to the future. With Love, Brian." Does this sound like a man bent on suicide?

EPILOGUE

TRACES OF DIZ

Ironically, the first steps to decriminalizing homosexuality in the UK were taken on July 27, 1967, a month before Brian's death. Before 1967, gay men could be jailed and given prison sentences of up to two years under the 'gross indecency laws.' Those legal changes only applied to England and Wales at the time.

Homosexuality was finally legalized in Scotland in 1980 and Northern Ireland in 1981.

The United States legalized sexual activity between consenting same-sex adults, as well as between consenting adolescents close in age, as legal acts across our nation on June 26, 2003.

Larry never found out what happened to Diz Gillespie after Brian's death, and he never heard from him again. It's as if the world just swallowed Diz up and never spit him out.

Our research found through one or more of our Federal contacts that no record exists for Diz Gillespie. No information has surfaced on his whereabouts. Perhaps the FBI and Scotland Yard do know the details of his existence? We are left to believe that he could have been placed in a witness protection program, or perhaps he was a confidential informant, exempting him from any investigations. But again, we are not sure, and it leaves all of this under great suspicion.

Did the Kray twins arrange a little visit to Brian over that weekend? In December of 1968, a year after death, Brian's music lawyer and friend David Jacobs, was found dead under suspicious circumstances. David was found hanging by a satin rope from a beam in his garage after he reportedly turned down a request to represent the Kray twins at their double murder trials.

Was there a connection between Brian and David's death? There were many similarities. They were both gay men; both were under pressure from the maniacal Kray twins; and both were powerful men in the entertainment business. They were both victims of blackmail and extortion, both were heavy users of amphetamines, and they both died under suspicious circumstances, their deaths were made to look like suicides.

Diz Gillespie was not a fictional character, nor was he a figment of imagination. There were plenty of people close to Brian that knew of and had interactions with him. Peter Brown, Brian's personal assistant, wrote of Diz in his book *The Love You Make*. Lonnie Trimble, Brian's valet, knew of and met Diz several times in London. His interviews concerning Diz are in the public record. Nat Weiss was a dear friend of Brian and his American music business lawyer. Diz stole his briefcase along with Brian's during the Beatles 1965 tour in America. Nat managed to locate Diz, who returned the briefcases minus their contents. Nat also met with Diz. Brian's parents both met Diz at a dinner in Brian's home.

Recently Brian Epstein's family put up his address book for sale. The item, B30239 is described as "small leather bound pocket address and telephone book that was formerly owned and used by Brian Epstein. The book dates to 1967 and it consists of 57 pages of addresses and telephone number some of which are typed, some of which are in the hand of Brian Epstein and some which have been added by hand on behalf of Brian. The book contains a total of 404 entries, a selection of them are listed below. It comes directly from the family of Brian Epstein. It measures 10cm x 16cm (4 inches x 6.3 inches). The condition is very good plus. Additional images available on request."

What's most interesting is that under the letter 'S', handwritten in Brian's own hand, is the name, address and phone number of Stanton, Lauren. (The Beatles Brian Epstein's Address & Telephone Book (UK) (www.trade.co.uk) > product > b30239-the-beatlews-brian-epsteins-addr.)

On December 4, 2006, in Rockefeller Center, New York, Christie's auctioned two items related to Brian Epstein; a copy of John Lennon's book *In His Own Write*, and an original 1962 Beatles handbill. The stated vendor was Diz. The notes pertaining to the handbill noted "the item was given to the vendor by Brian Epstein in 1966. The two had met at a party in Los Angeles in 1964." Christie's notes regarding the book state, "the vendor first met John Lennon and Brian Epstein in 1964 when he visited him at his home, Kenwood, Weybridge, Surrey. Diz was the vendor's nickname." Did this mean that Diz was alive in 2006 and still making money from Brian? (https://eppylover.livejournal.com/202432)

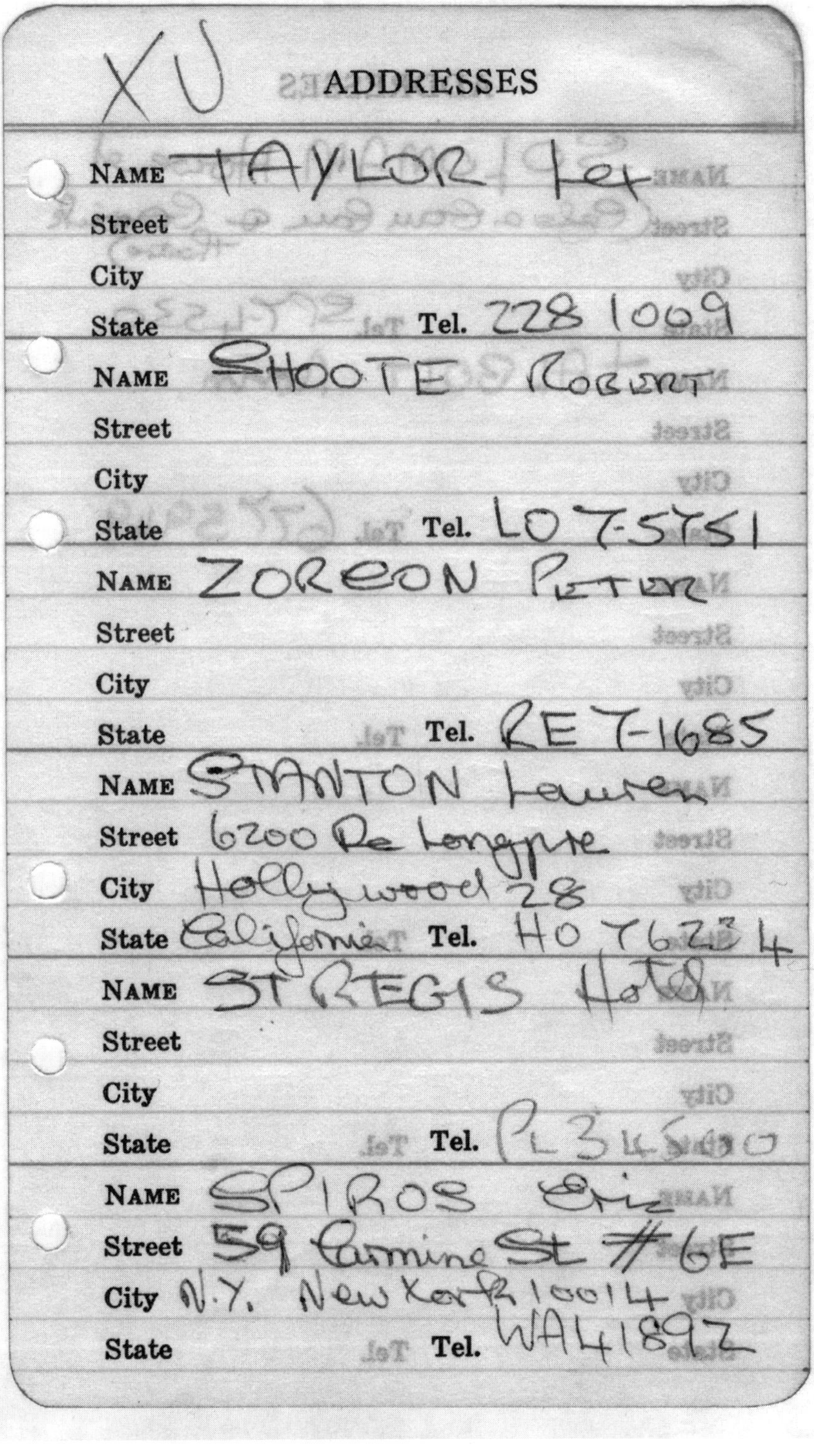

XU ADDRESSES

NAME TAYLOR Jet

Street

City

State   Tel. 228 1009

NAME SHOOTE ROBERT

Street

City

State   Tel. LO 7-5751

NAME ZOREON PETER

Street

City

State   Tel. RE 7-1685

NAME STANTON Lauren

Street 6200 Re Longpre

City Hollywood 28

State California   Tel. HO 7 6234

NAME ST REGIS Hotel

Street

City

State   Tel. PL 3 5500

NAME SPIROS Eric

Street 59 Carmine St #6E

City N.Y. New York 10014

State   Tel. WA 41892

Index

Hamburger Hamlet 11, 12
Harvey, Laurence 45, 49
HELP (Movie) 61, 74, 113
Herman's Hermits 61
Hilton, Francesca 35
Hoch, Max 89
Hollywood vii, 3, 5-7, 9-11, 22-25, 27-31,
    33, 35, 38, 39, 41, 45-47, 51-55, 59,
    63, 65, 69, 73, 74, 77, 78, 90, 93
Hollywood Bowl 51, 52
Hollywood Ranch Market 77, 78
Hollywood Reporter 24, 27
Holt, Leslie 83
Hoover, J. Edgar 103
Horn, Paul 89

I

In His Own Write 116

J

Jacobs, David 115
Jarrard, Rick 89
Johnson, Lyndon B. 51

K

Kennedy, John F. 3
Kitt, Eartha 78
Kramer, Billy J. 2, 12, 13
Kray brothers 81, 82, 84, 91, 98, 99, 111
Kray, Reggie 82, 99
Kray, Ronnie 82, 83, 98
Kray twins 17, 18, 81-84, 97, 99, 101,
    113, 115

L

La Rue Restaurant 27
La Scala Restaurant 36, 38, 63
Lennon, Cynthia 34
Lennon, John 10, 14, 29, 34, 49, 61, 79,
    103, 116
Lewis, Harry 11
Lewis, Marilyn 11
Livingston, Alan 29, 62, 78
Boothby, Robert (Lord) 82-84, 100,
    103

Love You Make, The 116
LSD vii, 7, 8, 41, 42, 45, 62, 63
Lyles, A.C. 38

M

Macmillan, Harold 83
Maharishi Mahesh Yogi 109
Manne, Shelly 6
Marcus, Greil 91
Martin, Dean 6, 7
Martoni's 55
McCartney, Paul 91, 109
Melody Room 53
MI5 83, 84, 100
Mineo, Sal viii, 30, 36, 37, 53, 55, 61-63
Musso & Frank 73, 74

N

Napier-Bell, Simon 95
NEMS (North End Music Stores) 29,
    31, 32, 65, 66, 91
Niklas, Kurt 78

O

Our Gang 38
Owen, Reginald 51

P

Pandora's Box 24
Parker, Tom 46, 49
Pennington, Richard (Little Richard)
    61
Perez, Manuel Benitez 34
Philbin, Regis 77, 78
Polo Lounge 49, 75
Presley, Elvis 46, 49, 50

Q

R

RCA 89
Rebel Without A Cause 30
Red Raven 38
Regis Philbin Television Show 77

Reprise (record label) 5, 9

S

Sands Hotel 56, 57, 59
Sanicola, Henry "Hank" 5, 9, 79
Schultz, Charles 100
Schwab's Pharmacy 23, 24
Scotland Yard 99, 100, 101, 107, 108,
    111, 115
Shelly's Manne-Hole 5, 6, 9
Sinatra, Frank viii, 5, 7, 9, 55, 57
Stanton, Larry ii, 1, 3, 5, 13, 22, 39, 59,
    116
Stigwood, Robert 91, 97
Sunday Express 83
Sunday Mirror 83
Supremes 3

T

Taylor, Alastair 91
Taylor, Derek 54, 73, 79
Telegraph 84
Tiny Naylor's 3
Trimble, Lonnie 66, 67, 69-71, 81, 90,
    116

U

UCLA 7, 12

V

Valentine Recording Studios 6
Venet, Nik 89
Villa Nova, The 53, 54

W

Walker, Gerald "Jerry" 3, 6-8, 10, 11,
    24, 39, 41, 69, 85, 87
Wallich's Music City 28, 29, 47
Washington, Diana 64
Weber, Andrew Lloyd 13
Weed, Gene 55
Weiss, Nat 85-87, 114, 116
Whiskey A Go-Go 11
Wilkerson, Bill 27

Wood, Natalie 30
Wrecking Crew 5

Y

Yellow Cab Company 6, 9, 25

Z

ACKNOWLEDGMENTS

We thank our family who supported us throughout this journey: Daughters; Natasha, Lexi and Nikki,

Greg & Trina Bragg, John & Diane Bragg, Renee Arroyo, Joanne Arroyo.

Camille & Alan & Dino Tanzillo, Kiki Sammarcelli, Brennan & Judith & Jasper

We especially thank Denis McCallion & Jenny Jones for their life long friendship, support, encouragement, and reminding us that "its not how you start the race but how you finish the race."

Thank you Geoff & Toni Miles for your friendship and creative guidance.

Thank you Joe Wallenstein for your friendship, thoughts, and encouragement

Thank you Robert (Kris) Millegan, our Publisher, for not giving up on us and guiding us through the creative writing and publishing process.

Thank you Howard Wolf for your friendship and wisdom,

Thank you Michael Sherry for your British insight.

Thank you St. John Hunt for your creative thoughts, ideas, and editing expertise.

Thank you Jimmy Wachtel and Wolfie for their life long friendship and support, and for creating our Book cover.

Dr. Ernest Bragg, Roberta Bragg, Keith White and Julio B. Sammarcelli, Caroline Sammarcelli for their inspiration.

And to Larry Stanton a very special thank you for his friendship and trust for allowing us to tell his story.